T0340394

Advance Praise

Working with Payal was a delightful experience. She impressed us with her passion, diligence, sharp intellect, commitment, optimism, and perseverance. She is a good communicator who readily connects with her target audience through cogent presentations, meaningful content, and persuasive delivery. I unhesitatingly recommend Payal's work.

Payal has beautifully defined success as to "reach where you want from where you are." She emphasizes rightful karma or focused execution to keep you on the right path so that you are always walking in a direction that takes you toward your goal.

Her stories explain how our inner thoughts are a source of powerful energy. Positivity begets positive outcomes and negativity spells doom. The nature conspires to help us realize our deepest thoughts. Our positive mind-sets will manifest into happiness and success. Similarly, the negative thoughts will result in further negativity and failures.

Payal stresses the significance of karma in life. It is well known that nature always gives us a choice. We are more likely to exercise the right option if we are at peace with ourselves and pick the wrong alternative when the mindset is strained. The results we get are in line with the choices we make.

She has an easy and effective narrative that simplifies the complex karmic philosophy and brings it within the grasp of all readers. As we sow, so shall we harvest is the lesson.

This book emphasizes the possibilities of mental control. Payal believes that all human beings can train themselves for inner strength to make themselves happy, satisfied, and successful.

Dr. Arun Arora, CEO, EDVANCE

This book is full of practical tips on how to become a successful leader and the best part is Payal has narrated it wonderfully with appropriate fables and relevant case studies. Payal's system of coaching, Leadership Through Mind, is very effective and is full of interactive activities and games. Her passion, enthusiasm, and sincerity are apparent in her coaching sessions and I can see the same in the book as well. I was privileged to work with Payal for the Inner Power Leadership (IPL) Series. Her entrepreneurial attitude and impactful wisdom are commendable and evident in the IPL series.

Swapna Hari, Director, Cognizant

External success is always very sweet, and we all want double helpings of it. But while pursuing it, we invariably miss the point. It is our inner victories, which lay the foundation for outer accomplishment. This book by Payal Nanjiani will join the best of business literature for emphasizing attitude as our biggest asset. By virtue of her experience as an executive coach and leadership trainer, Payal has developed very useful tools for mind management. These techniques are systematically laid out in the book, making it a very practical guide for enriching the quality of our thoughts, emotions, and actions.

Swami Mukundananda of Jagadguru Kripaluji Yog (JKYog) Institute

Payal Nanjiani has attacked the most important problem of this era in how to get better results by doing less, or in doing things in a new and different way. Society is in constant catch up/keep up mode. Payal's book gives us techniques using what we all have—our minds—to keep us grounded, keep us focused, and to enable us to function at a high level with consistent input. I highly encourage those ready to take on the business world full speed to read this book and think about leveraging their minds to enable success.

Ramona Jackson, Senior Director IT Strategy, Planning and Governance,Ciena

I know Payal Nanjiani as an inspirational speaker and leader. Her approach to leadership and "transforming your mindset" was a game-changer for me. This book will compel you to recognize and harness your energy to become a better leader. The illustration of her strategies through real-life scenarios paired with fables is engaging and fun. This book is a must read.

Donna Daniels, Program Manager, SAS

SUCCESS IS WITHIN

SUCCESS IS WITHIN

The 21 Ways for Achieving Results, Prosperity, and Fulfillment by Changing Your Leadership Mindset

PAYAL NANJIANI

A BIBLIOMOTION BOOK

Routledge/Bibliomotion, Inc.
52 Vanderbilt Avenue, 11th Floor New York, NY 10017
2 Park Square, Milton Park, Abingdon, Oxon OX14 4RN, UK

Routledge/Bibliomotion is an imprint of Taylor & Francis Group, an Informa business

No claim to original U.S. Government works

Printed on acid-free paper

International Standard Book Number-13: 978-0-367-23267-2 (Hardback)
International Standard Book Number-13: 978-0-367-23263-4 (Paperback)

This book contains information obtained from authentic and highly regarded sources. Reasonable efforts have been made to publish reliable data and information, but the author and publisher cannot assume responsibility for the validity of all materials or the consequences of their use. The authors and publishers have attempted to trace the copyright holders of all material reproduced in this publication and apologize to copyright holders if permission to publish in this form has not been obtained. If any copyright material has not been acknowledged please write and let us know so we may rectify in any future reprint.

Library of Congress Cataloging-in-Publication Data

Names: Nanjiani, Payal, author.
Title: Success is within: the 21 ways for achieving results, prosperity, and fulfillment by changing your leadership mindset / Payal Nanjiani.
Description: 1 Edition. | New York: Taylor & Francis, [2019] | Includes bibliographical references and index.
Identifiers: LCCN 2019005324 (print) | LCCN 2019006938 (ebook) | ISBN 9780429279041 (e-Book) | ISBN 9780367232634 (pbk.: alk. paper) | ISBN 9780367232672 (hardback: alk. paper)
Subjects: LCSH: Leadership. | Thought and thinking. | Strategic planning. | Success in business.
Classification: LCC HD57.7 (ebook) | LCC HD57.7 .N356 2019 (print) | DDC 658.4/092—dc23
LC record available at https://lccn.loc.gov/2019005324

Visit the Taylor & Francis Web site at
http://www.taylorandfrancis.com

Most of all, to my husband, Ashish Nanjiani,
who is a living example of unconditional love and support.
This book has been his dream for years.

Contents

Preface

Are you where you want to be in your career? Have you gained accomplishments, yet you are still full of stress and worry? Your hard work is paying off. You are doing well in your field. You have the skills and knowledge. But even with this progress, you aren't where you want to be. There is something standing between you and the next level of achievement.

This book helps you transform your habits to achieve unstoppable success. I am an executive coach who has interacted with professionals in Fortune 500 corporations, medium-sized organizations, and small businesses around the globe. Some of these professionals long for success, yet fail to achieve what they want. Other leaders and entrepreneurs are able to quickly build thriving businesses and move from one success to the next.

How is that possible? What is missing? I've found that the secret lies in their minds. I have become a *business whisperer* who gives professionals vital strategies to elevate their careers by transforming their mindset. I call my system of leadership coaching "Success Is Within."

This book is about making leadership and success easy and attainable for everyone. All you have to do is transform your mind. My seminars, trainings, and coaching sessions help busy professionals reach their highest levels of success. My coaching inspires to transform: I help professionals transform information into action so that they bridge the gap between where they are and where they want to be. I guide them to transform themselves with speed and serenity.

The core of this book presents 21 *karmas*—or actions—that you can do to boost your career. Understanding the word "karma" is central to the book. Karma is an Indian word that has become common in the United States. Many people think that karma only means retribution—or, what comes around goes around. But when I use the word karma, I refer to its original meaning from Ancient Sanskrit: karma simply means "action." Our actions are reciprocal. They flow from the way we think: from our mind.

Thus, this book is about attuning our minds with specific karmas—or actions. In my description of the word karma, you no doubt discerned that I am one of the many professionals who have come to the United States from other countries to make their fortune and contribute to the American dream. After a successful business career in my home country of India, I came to America and founded my own executive coaching company. Today, I travel all over the world helping busy professionals at many different kinds of organizations to unblock barriers to success so that they achieve prosperity.

The prevailing myth is that success comes from external factors. The truth is that real success comes from within. Rather than giving you solutions to solve outer issues, this book gives you techniques to enhance your state of mind. As leaders, we have many goals. Our goals often go unrealized because of a lack of self-awareness. To improve your chances of reaching your goals with speed and serenity, at every step it is imperative to stop and self-reflect. During my trainings, seminars, and coaching, I give ample time for people to self-reflect so that when they leave, they feel accomplished and see their results manifesting.

Today's modern workplace is all about the "doing." Everywhere you see people who are focused on doing. They are constantly engaged in some outer action to achieve something. Most of us have pushed ourselves to the limit and are sucked into a career. We have become slaves to the clock, and our lives are centered on work. We have neglected the *being* in favor of the doing.

There are two states in which you can achieve your results: a demagnetized state or a magnetized state. People who come to work with a focus only on the doing, or solely on the results, are in a demagnetized state. While in this state, the person is surrounded by stress, anxiety, fear, and self-doubt. He does not use his full potential. He is self-critical. Results are usually sporadic in nature. Even if the person manages to get continuous results, it comes at the cost of a healthy body and mind. His unhealthy state slows down growth.

In contrast, the person who works with focus on both the being and the doing is in a magnetized state. Here the person is full of confidence, healthy self-belief, joy, and serenity. This person will move ahead even in times of adversity and failure achieving continuous results, both internally and externally.

One of my strategies in this book is to offer true-life stories from my work with my coaching clients. I pair these true-life stories with classic fables and inspirational tales from around the world. My goal is to illustrate the strategies that I suggest to you with a rich tapestry of storytelling. Let me pause and tell you a story that will help you understand why this book may be the only one that you need to gain unstoppable success.

A king was touring his kingdom on his elephant. Suddenly he stopped in front of a shop in the market and said to his minister, "I don't know why, but I want to hang the owner of this shop." The minister was shocked.

The next day, the minister went to that shop dressed as one of the locals to meet the shopkeeper. He casually asked him how his business was progressing. The shopkeeper, a sandalwood merchant, reported sadly that he had hardly any customers. People would come to his shop, smell the sandalwood, and then go away. They would even praise the quality of the sandalwood but rarely buy anything. His only hope was that the king would die soon. Then there would be a huge demand for sandalwood for performing his last rites. As he was the only sandalwood merchant around, he was sure the king's death would mean a windfall.

The minister now understood why the king had expressed a desire to kill the shopkeeper. Perhaps, the shopkeeper's negative thought had subtly affected the king, who had, in turn, felt the same kind of negative thought arising within his self.

The shopkeeper nurtured a negative thought toward the king because of losses in his business. He meant well, but he was full of avarice and disappointment, and his body became numb to the actions of not working hard. The minister realized that the problem was a matter of the mind: the shopkeeper's negativity had not only made him lose business, but it had also attracted the ire of the king.

Though you absolutely have a positive purpose for achieving your outcome, your mind, actions, and sentiments are often disturbed. A mind that is filled with tension will create what type of results? Yes: the answer is poor results. We want happiness and great results, but we are full of tension.

You take yourself with you everywhere. This means that if you feel successful, you take success with you everywhere, and if you feel like a failure, you take failure with you everywhere. If you carry negativity, you carry it with you to your workplace. It is on each of us to create the work environment we hope for. It starts with YOU. Get ready to look within and create the wave of change in your results! Let's go for it.

Acknowledgments

This work is a synergistic product of many great minds. For the development of this book, I feel a deep sense of gratitude:

To my parents—my mother, Laltoo Malkani, and my father, Ashok Malkani, both who gave me an unconditional love and courage to keep moving ahead at all times, including during times of struggle. My mother has always encouraged me to do my very best and leave the rest to destiny. Whatever my mother does she does in the mode of happiness, and her joyfulness has enriched my life and this book. My father supported me in my career journey. He encouraged me to step outside my own boundaries. At all times he is a constant source of inspiration.

To my aunt, Meenu Shivani from whom I learnt the value of being an independent woman and the importance of challenging yourself constantly regardless of age.

To my deceased uncle, Manik Shivani, who inspired me to develop a strong will power in times of challenges. I miss you and hope you would have seen this book come alive.

To my loving and supportive husband, Ashish Nanjiani without whom this book would not have been possible, and to my two lovely daughters—Ronisha and Rishona—who constantly stand beside me in all my endeavors.

To my loving "Anni" family who have always embraced me and showered their love on me.

To my *Success Is Within* team, for their loyalty and dedication on every project and assignment to ensure that each client gets the best leadership content and service from us.

To my clients—both small to medium businesses and Fortune 500 companies—who trust in me and in the Success Is Within leadership techniques. This book is a proof of the success you all have achieved by applying these techniques.

To my mentors and advisors who have guided me in my career, and a big thank you to Cleis Abeni.

To Routledge and the Taylor & Francis Group for trusting in me and making this book reach its highest potential.

Most importantly, to the higher power, the universe, that guides all hopes and magnifies all good things.

Author

Payal Nanjiani is one of the world's few Indian-American globally acclaimed motivational leadership speakers, executives and business coaches, and CEO of *Success Is Within* Leadership, Inc. Payal Nanjiani has risen to global prominence by delivering a high-energy leadership wisdom which tells people that success in the corporate and business world can be achieved with both speed and serenity regardless of the circumstance or economy. It is a message Payal Nanjiani has learned from her own life and one which she brings to her clients to help them attain success.

For over two decades, she has not only studied the science of success, but also mastered it by interviewing and collaborating with successful business leaders, translating theory into bottom line results for her clients. She is known for spreading leadership wisdom, the most needed element today for success in the corporate and business world. As a result, companies are witnessing a massive shift in their teams' actions and results.

Payal also works with organizations and CEOs to develop game-changing leaders and create a culture that improves both productivity and profits. Her work can be seen in Fortune 500 companies as well as in small to medium businesses. She has helped organizations develop world-class coaches within their companies.

She has been featured on television, global magazines, radio talk shows, podcasts, and more. She is a regular guest speaker on America's radio show.

Payal lives her motto—"Success Is Within" and believes that success can be achieved with speed and serenity in any economy.

To know more about her work and to connect with her, visit www.payalnanjiani.com or email success@payalnanjiani.com.

Success Is Within Coaching

As a result of Success Is Within coaching, executives, entrepreneurs, women, and individual contributors have been able to successfully navigate the realities of the workplace with speed and serenity. In today's high-pressure work environment, Success Is Within coaching has a direct and positive impact on your behavior, actions, and results. It transforms you deeply from within and you become a master of your game. Payal is known for helping her clients achieve their results within five coaching sessions.

Success Is Within Workshops

Companies and individuals are witnessing a massive positive and lasting change in the behavior of their employees and an increase in their financial outcomes as a result of the Success Is Within workshops. Innovation and speed of implementation has improved massively. Corporate teams and leaders are now able to intentionally and consciously define, articulate, and influence their self-leadership and interpersonal leadership toward achieving greater outcomes.

Would you want to bring these results to your company? Reach out to Payal and her team at success@payalnanjiani.com

Payal is known to inspire leaders and teams through her workshops and has transformed the lives of men and women, developing numerous game-changing leaders and entrepreneurs globally.

Success Is Within for Women

Payal has customized corporate programs to support women's leadership efforts in the workplace. Programs are designed to align with the specific goals and needs of the organization and are often initially delivered with a live workshop and a follow-up virtual or live group coaching support. She has a customized coaching program for women entrepreneurs designed to encourage women to think more strategically about their careers, build strategic relationships, and clarify their value proposition. In the market, Payal has significantly enhanced the economic achievements of thousands of women globally, encouraging them to climb the corporate ladder, succeed in business, and realize their true potential. Her podcast channel, "iSucceed," is dedicated to inspiring women in jobs and business.

Introduction: Achieve Unstoppable Success

The difference between a peak performer and an average performer is your karma—your actions. In turn, your karma is based on your state of mind. Whatever takes place in your professional life is a result of your actions—your karmas. What you put in or put out, you get back. If you are successful today, then it's because of the actions you have taken in the past that brought you to where you are today. So, wherever you are is because of your own karmas. You create a karmic account every day when you interact with people, work on a project, plan, and think.

Your karma—your action—flows from your mindset. A disturbed mindset leads to poor actions, and an enriched mindset leads to massively successful actions. For success and prosperity, it is important to condition your mind in a way that leads you to your desired outcome. A mindset conditioned to success will undertake actions that lead to prosperity.

Mantras help us to condition the mindset. They are sayings that we repeat to ourselves to deepen our positive inner awareness. One ancient, powerful mantra that creates an especially positive vibe the minute you say it is "Om." This two-letter word approximates the low guttural vibration of our deepest thoughts and the metaphorical sound of our smallest, unseen, subatomic inner energies.

Chanting *Om* purifies the environment around you and helps foster a deeper connection to the self. It actually makes you realize the infinite power you have within you to achieve unstoppable success in any situation at work. Stop right now and simply say the word a few times and feel the vibration within your mouth, throat, and nasal passages. Let the energy create by this vibration permeate through you and create waves of calm. When you activate your inner self in this manner, you drive to the root of your being and awaken your inner positivity. Let's turn now to a fuller description of "the root," or our inner drive.

The Root

There is a buzzword going around in the professional world. Everyone talks about it. People want to see it in others. Management and leaders push their teams toward it. Teams look up to their management and role models for it. Amateurs lack it. Achievers say they possess it in abundance. Success is dependent on it. It is within each person, but only a few actually use it to the fullest. Any guesses what it is? The buzzword is "inner drive."

We've all been there. We really want to do that project. We know it makes sense for us to wake up early. We know hard work and discipline matter. Yet, we find ourselves procrastinating. We have fallen into a trap, and we can't find our way out. This is because we operate in a work culture where we are only results-oriented robots. Numbers and achievement judge everything. Now this does not mean that results aren't important. Don't get me wrong please. Results are very important because they take us closer to our goals and achievements. In my coaching sessions and workshops, I help people design results with complete clarity.

If results are truly important, and if everything depends on numbers and outcomes, then we should place more emphasis on the human *being* rather than the human doing. Ultimately, it is the being that achieves truly lasting results. If you look around today, we talk about mindfulness, yoga, healthy diet, great benefits, work life balance, opportunities, and innovations. But in the midst of all this, the person's being is actually unhappy, stressed, and full of worry, anxiety, dissatisfaction, greed, doubt, and negativity.

Most successful entrepreneurs and leaders have an awareness of what it took to get there. I was once dining with Clark, the CEO of a well-known chain of restaurants, and his friend Scott, who had come to meet him. At that time, I was working at Clark's company as the Human Resource Head. Just before Clark could join us, Scott spilled a little bit of his drink on the floor and said to me, "I bet Clark will get a tissue to wipe this, wash his hands, and then join us." I did not believe it as Clark had many servers and janitors to do this for him. But to my amazement, Clark did just what Scott told me.

"Payal, did I not win the bet?" Scott looked at me and said when Clark joined us for dinner. "Do you know that Clark and I started our career in the restaurant industry together? We encountered the same opportunities and obstacles along the way. Isn't that funny? But what I hate most is that today Clark is the owner of a chain of 35 restaurants and here I am working as just a vice president in a hotel. I aspired to own restaurants. My career life hasn't been fair at all to me."

I nodded in agreement. Clark smiled, sipped his beer, and said, "No, Scott, life has been fair to both of us. Remember the time we both got our first jobs as interns in a small hotel?" Scott nodded in agreement as we both listened thoughtfully. Clark continued with a smile. "One night, the hotel we worked in got a huge catering order for a graduation event. We both were given the responsibility to ensure that everything went smoothly and we both completed our responsibility excellently.

"That night we wrapped up everything, and around 11:30 pm, we started to drive toward our home together. On the way I told you that I felt we had left one trash bag in the hallway, and we should go back and dispose of it. You said, it's okay, that someone would dispose of it by the morning and that it was too tiring to drive back just for one trash bag. That night, my dear friend, you went to your home and slept peacefully, but I drove back, disposed of the trash bag, and came home around 1 am. I then slept peacefully."

Scott breathed deeply. I was lost in their conversation. Even today, Clark's commitment remained the same.

"Scott, I am where I am and you are where you are today because of your own actions and thoughts," Clark said to Scott. "That night I not only had a full stomach, I was also enriched in my mind because I learned a huge lesson about career life. The difference between people who make it and those who don't is only our actions (our karmas) based on our mindset."

You can always tell who owns a business by who does even the menial jobs. The deeper the root of the tree, the better the fruits. Whether you are an entrepreneur, CEO, engineer, surgeon, painter, hairstylist, homemaker, you are the root of your success and failure. Your actions will determine your future. So, it's imperative that this root is taken care of, because it will bear the fruits, and these fruits will help the coming workforce generation to stand strong and achieve more than what seems possible. If you do not focus on what is unseen (your mindset), you will be disappointed with what's seen—"the results." Take a moment and ask yourself, "Am I a root leader or a fruit leader?"

Leaders who simply focus on results don't do nearly as well as those who also pay attention to the root. Every tree has three aspects: root, trunk, and crown. For a tree to stand firm, green, and full of fruits, its roots must be deeply spread and well nourished. This tree will be able to endure strong winds and stand firm in the midst of climatic changes. Take care of the roots and the fruits will take care of themselves. If you do not focus on what is unseen (the root, or the state of mind), you will be disappointed with what is seen (the fruits or the results).

Similarly, for your career life to be successful, there are three essentials: your mindset (root), your karma (trunk), and your results (fruits). If you want the fruits, you must take care of the roots. All karma at the workplace is because of the mindset. As the mind, so the karma.

Today corporate leaders and business owners are focusing heavily on the fruits to stay ahead of the game, which is leading to stress, negativity, less creativity, low energy, unproductivity, limited results, and

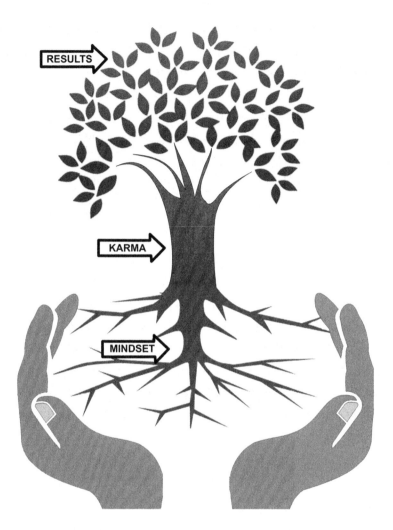

high staff turnover. They operate in a demagnetized state. To outlast and manifest massive results in times of rapid changes, innovation, disruption, and market transitions, you must take care of the roots, which are for the most part invisible. Take care of the roots, and the fruits will take care of themselves.

I repeat: If you do not focus on what is unseen (mindset), you will be disappointed with what's seen—"the results." Take a moment and ask yourself, "Am I a root leader or a fruit leader?" A fruit leader is merely attracted to the fruits (results) and focuses only on the doing while neglecting the being. A root leader is also attracted to the fruits (results), but focuses largely on the being. This leader integrates the doing and the being. Now you may ask, what is the whole point of doing anything if we aren't focusing on the results? Let's explore this thought.

Say, for example, you want to become the director of a company or want to close a deal with a potential client. This is the result you want to produce. But for reasons unknown you don't produce the result. If you are a fruit leader, you focus profoundly on the results and the doing. You will be frustrated and disturbed, losing your serenity because you did not achieve the results. You will criticize yourself and beat yourself up categorizing yourself as a "non-achiever." You may even give up. On the other hand, if you are a root leader, your focus is largely on your actions (karmas) and your mindset (root). Even when you do not achieve the results, you are stimulated to move ahead and look for opportunities. You will bounce back sooner from failures and disappointments. You will have the strength to move from one project to another with speed and serenity. And isn't success all about moving ahead? Root leaders know the result they desire and then work from the mindset and karmas. They integrate the being and the doing.

The state in which we operate today, the challenges a leader faces, and the number of potentially difficult decisions that have to be made in a limited amount of time can be daunting. Chances are a wind of layoffs, economic downturn, budgetary challenges, and staff problems might blow, and uproot us. Nourishing your root (mind) is more crucial than ever. Fruits (results) are essential, no doubt. However, fruits must be sustained and must be sweet. For this, the roots must be well nourished. The major reason there is a gap between where you are and where you want to be is because you oscillate between the outcome and action forgetting to go deeper down and take corrective actions at the mindset level. Once you condition yourself at the mindset level, the karmas and results align.

Like the tree, your success has three essentials. I call it the 3D essentials of success: design, dynamic, and deliverables.

1. Design your outcome (Results).
2. Build a dynamic you (Mindset).
3. Achieve deliverables (Action).

Sophia's Equations

Today's modern workplace is all about the doing. Everywhere around, you see people are over-focused on their workplace performance. Let me give you an example. Sophia had just moved from Connecticut to New Jersey to take up a job with an advertising firm. She worked hard to create a financially secure and satisfying life. After years of college and business management school, and working late nights and weekends, she finally secured an enviable position in a top advertising firm as a Managing Director at the age of 31. Many envy her seven-figure salary and luxurious New York City home on a downtown Manhattan street.

I knew Sophia for more than 12 years. We first met when we were in business management school. Even then she seemed to have it all. She was brilliant at her job and beautiful for her age. She dreamed of success and wanted to be a peak performer.

But one day I met Sophia not at her classy office, but in a hospital room. Sophia was admitted there for a mild heart attack that caught her in the middle of a critical business deal. When I saw Sophia in the hospital bed, she was dictating a letter to her assistant who typed it up promptly on a laptop.

"You weren't working, were you?" I asked Sophia after her assistant left her hospital room.

"Of course I was, Payal," Sophia confirmed. "There is an important letter that needs to go out today to a client and if I miss it, the deadline is gone." That day Sophia did not look enthusiastic.

"We are all caught up in this hyper-competitive career world," Sophia told me, "and it has taken a toll on many, both physically and emotionally. Our jobs are fast-paced environments, and our demands are endless. We keep up this pace, but our doctors tell us to slow down.

How will we achieve our goals if we slow down in this fast-paced career-world?" There was silence in the room as Sophia and I looked at each other.

Sophia was undoubtedly successful. She achieved in her career what most people only dreamed about. But did her success have to come at the cost of her being unhealthy? Do we have to get to a point where we are given an ultimatum to either give up our dreams or give up our health? Do we have to visit the hospital or come to the brink of being in the funeral home to pause and reflect on ourselves?

Let's think of Sophia's struggle as an equation. In business, we often deploy logical thinking and so much of our success is measured in equivalences. Thinking in terms of equations may help us tap into the thought processes that animate our business cultures. Sophia's results (R), both positive and negative, are because of Sophia's doing (D). The doing is because of the being (B). So results are because of the being. Here is Sophia's equation:

$$\text{If } R = D \text{ and } D = B \text{ then } R = B$$

The being has to engage in better karmas—better actions—to achieve results. Sophia worked hard to create a financially secure and satisfying life, completing college and business management school, working late nights and weekends, and even working while in the hospital. Out of these, some of her karmas were conducive, and some were not. When we focus on being, we foster happiness, strong emotional development, and positive relationships with self and others. This is the fruit of the karma of happiness and success.

In this era of innovative technology, people have tremendous access to knowledge, resources, and opportunities. Yet, despite these things, according to statistics from the University of Scranton and the Statistic Brain Research Institute, only 8 percent of people who set New Year's goals actually achieve them. There is something significant missing in our professional world. And that significant something is *being*.

The being (B) is made up of mindset and karma. Results (R) are because of being as seen in the earlier equation. Our mindset (M)—the way that we think within our being—leads to certain karmas (K). Success and failure (results) are a series of karmic cycles that we create daily based on our mindset. This can be expressed in the following equations:

$$\text{If } B = M + K \text{ and } R = B$$

$$\text{Then } R = M + K$$

I believe this equation has a compounding effect. It builds up and spreads around you. Let's look at another simple example to understand the equation. Suppose you spoke angrily with a colleague in your office, "You're always late to the office. When are you going to understand the importance of being on time?" Every karma has consequences. By speaking angrily, you have disturbed your state of mind. Due to your state of mind (angry and disturbed), your words are harsh. Now look at what follows.

When your colleague leaves, this state continues within you and him. You are likely to talk about this issue with others. Merely thinking about this colleague disturbs your state of mind. In this state, the next decisions you make and the actions you take will influence your results. Your results were primarily because of your mindset (M) and karma (K). It also affects your colleague who feels he isn't appreciated and wishes he had another boss. So his results also drop and overall, the company is affected.

Happy Karma

Let's take another example. Suppose you are super happy because of a deal you just signed. Your state of mind is at its peak, and during this time you make a few calls to potential clients. Because of this state of mind, you are engaging in an insightful conversation that leads to the client meeting. In this state, the decisions you make and the actions you take positively influence your results. Your client also feels great dealing with a person like you, and it enhances his day too. Your results are primarily because of your mindset and karma.

We often forget to attend to our karmas during our daily work routine. We blame situations and people and block our way to success. Maybe this is one reason I usually hear from business owners and employees that their work life is like a battlefield. Many people feel that every day is like a war and they dislike fighting. And for some of us, it is a long journey.

We get tired of corporate politics, cold calls, marketing the business, climbing the success ladder, networking, dealing with clients, receiving and giving negative feedback, endless targets, continuous deadlines, workplace gossip, negativity at work, dodging layoffs, and many daily battles. Career life is both a struggle and a constant journey, and you are a mighty warrior and traveler. In this battlefield, there is success and failure, gaining and losing. If you slow down or leave mid-way, it will do no good. In fact, your inner voice will condemn you, and you would not have performed your duty to the fullest.

Your mindset and karma are the most powerful tools you have on the road to triumph. Balanced mindset and karma are the main difference between why one person is successful and another a failure, why some climb the corporate ladder while others are stuck at a particular grade level, why some businesses flourish while others close, why some leaders are happy at work and others are unhappy, and why one manager is outstanding and another mediocre. It's all about the karma based on your mindset. A little work, just a little work—I promise—on your mindset will help you change your karmas and your results.

From Skill Set to Mindset

Today's business leaders are not first movers but fast movers. Everywhere around us there is change. So when everything is upgrading and releasing new versions, I ask you this: Have you updated and released a new version of yourself? Have you disrupted your old mental patterns? When was the last time you made a radically significant change in yourself that brought about a positive impact on your leadership? I am talking beyond skill set upgrades here. These are critical questions because we are in an era where skills are bountiful and increasingly outsourced. With rapid technology changes and robots replacing humans, today's skills may be obsolete tomorrow. Mindset separates the best from the rest. You must move from changing your skill set to changing your mindset. In this age of drones and artificial intelligence, how will you outsource a successful mindset that produces massive results?

Leadership is like a two-sided coin. On the one side is the skill set that helps you start and progress throughout your career. On the other side is the mindset that allows you to grow exponentially, tap into your inner potential, and experience massive success. However, when you only try to stay current with your skill set, you neglect your mindset. Skill set helps only the doing. Mindset helps both the being and doing. It is that hidden aspect which shows up in your results.

Think about this: Have you been curious about why your results are not in proportion to your efforts? Have you observed that many times you are stuck in a situation, and it seems impossible to get out of it? Have there been times when another person gained a competitive advantage over you? There are reasons behind these experiences. We are anxious to improve our situation and results. Any effort you put in with a goal in mind for the desired result has two main components: external and internal factors.

Internal factors are your emotions, energy, beliefs, and attitude—in short, your mindset. You can empower yourself to nourish your mindset. When it comes to the intrinsic factor, there is only one you. The internal situation can be altered the way you want. Once you change the internal situation, your outer condition will manifest according to the karmas that you have engaged. Your success at work depends on your skills of internal management. During the successful times, this internal management teaches you how to ensure sustainable growth.

During the unfortunate times, this internal management teaches you how to sustain yourself and move away from misfortune toward fortune.

Once, after conducting a workshop for a group of leaders and business owners, John, a senior manager of a Fortune 500 company, approached me and asked politely, "May I talk to you about an important matter?" I asked him to give me a few minutes. Later, we sat down to talk. The following is a close approximation of what he shared with me.

"I am working on a very crucial project for my company," John told me. "The success of this project ensures my growth in the company that has been stagnant for the past 5 years. I feel under tremendous pressure and have started to feel things are not going the way they should. I have been chosen for this project because I possess all the necessary skills to take it to the next level."

John and I spoke about this matter, and with some weeks of coaching, he applied the Success Is Within (LTM) principles. Today, he is the vice president of his company. Using these methods, he was able to experience exponential growth with speed and serenity within only a few years.

Here is another example of the effectiveness of Success Is Within principles. Several years ago, I got a chance to attend a sales meeting where I met two business owners of different companies in a similar industry. Beth and John were each presenting their franchise's proposal to a few buyers in the conference room. Both had strong projects and equally fluent presentational skills. After much debate and thought, the plan went in favor of Beth. After the buyers and business owners left, the executive of the sales committee turned to his team and said the following:

"Both are CEOs of different companies in the same industry, have similar qualifications, started their careers with almost the same circumstances, and today both had equally strong proposals. Why then did the buyers opt for Beth's proposal even when John was willing to negotiate some terms? Did Beth have more knowledge, education, money, health, people or time than John or any of us here?" he asked his team. The executive then proceeded to explain that the difference is only what the business leaders could glean about their mindsets. "Mindset precedes skill set in every aspect of life."

You may have the same skill set as others, but with a balanced mindset you can do more with those skills and learn new skills too. Mindset precedes skill set in every aspect of life. This thought has stayed with me. I have met people who do not have skill sets, but because they had a mindset conducive to success, their karmas led them to work toward attaining skill sets for their task.

On the other hand, I know leaders who have an array of skill sets, but aren't reaching anywhere with it. In the initial years of your career, you may require various skill sets. But soon your mindset takes over. The being and the doing integrate so that you reach the heights of success in your work.

You must cultivate a mindset that bridges the gap between reality and dreams. The more I interacted with people, the more profoundly I realized what makes some business owners, leaders, and individuals succeed. It was because of their balanced mindset and balanced karmas. Inner conditioning is what helps you maintain a steady mindset and karma.

The modern workplace has a diverse variety of personality types and a mixture of cultures. It has complicated disruptions and rapid changes. It is fast-paced, and there are endless demands. It has become more crucial than ever that businesses and professionals pause to nourish their mindset and upgrade their karmas to speed up again. The karmas in the following chapters will help you bring a definite shift in your mindset that will get you your desired results. The karmic cycle thus continues, bringing speed and serenity in your career life.

I have written this book with complete faith that it will help you in the time that you have. I believe that you are destined to win regardless of your circumstance. The only thing needed is for you to take absolute control over your karma and condition your mind for success. Whatever comes and goes in your professional life, you can take strength from within yourself, and trust yourself. I hope that this book serves as a guide to corporate leaders, individuals in their early careers, individuals at a crossroads in their careers, and business owners aspiring not only to win but to outlast their competition with serenity. Practicing these karmas will help you to not only survive but thrive in your job and business. This book and my thoughts have been inspired from my experience, the inspirational stories my father would share with me, stories from my mentors and teachers, as well as from scriptures like Vedas, the Bible, and Bhagavad Gita that I have grown up with.

KARMA 1

Mind the Mind

What did you have for breakfast this morning? I hope it was something healthy. There is a lot of research about the importance of starting your day with a healthy breakfast to boost your energy. But there is another kind of nourishing "breakfast" that you need every day. You also need to nourish the mind. You need to start your day off with healthy, optimistic, and constructive thoughts and feelings to produce great results in your career every day. Mind your mind: Fortify yourself internally for success.

When I say "mind," I am referring to the internal condition that we are in every single day. If this condition is optimal, then we will be stress free and emotionally grounded. The goal is for our inner actions to control our outer behavior. For more than two decades of coaching, I have met many business professionals and corporate leaders, but only a few have a planned daily "diet" for the mind to help them achieve their goals each day. The mind is most often neglected. Its care and nourishment is pushed aside because we think that we are too busy in our careers.

Consequently, many professionals are stressed out and emotionally drained because they are working with a chaotic and disturbed mind. A mind that isn't given proper attention will run wild and cause havoc in our lives. The uncontrolled mind is the sole source of fear, stress, and anger in our careers today. None of us knows what will transpire in our outer environment because we often have little or no control over it. But we can control our inner environment—we can control our minds. There are people who lose their job or their business becomes ruined, but, within themselves, they are still alive and well. Within their inner selves, they aren't finished. Within their minds, they aren't defeated.

I realized the importance of minding the mind when traveling to Dubai in the United Arab Emirates to deliver a 2-day corporate workshop. On the way to the session, I passed a shop that was burnt down, and there was nothing except debris. Above this debris, stood a small board with a big message. The board read, "My shop has been burnt down, but my commitment and dedication hasn't. I will bounce back soon." What a powerful message! Whatever happens in your career life, whether profit or loss, promotion or demotion, happiness or sadness, abundance or lack, prosperity or debt, you will always bounce back if you control your mind.

During the same trip to Dubai, I experienced another example of the importance of minding the mind. A client suddenly changed the location of our meeting to a hospital. After finalizing our work, I asked him why we met at a hospital. He told me that he had a mild heart attack because of the stress that he endured with a client of his own that had incurred many losses in his business. It was clear to me that my client's mind was compromised. This incident proved to me once again that we create the destiny of our own careers by minding the mind.

During times of turmoil as well as peace, it's the mind—our inner thoughts and feelings—that makes us or breaks us. It is very crucial to mind your mind. Chapter 6, Verses 5–6 of the *Bhagavad Gita* say the following: "A man must elevate himself by his own mind, not degrade himself. The mind is the friend of the conditioned soul, and his enemy as well. For him who has conquered the mind, the mind is the best of friends; but for one who has failed to do so his very mind will be the greatest enemy."

In my seminars, I share with participants an acronym I invented called "EAT." EAT stands for Events, Action, and Thoughts. Let me ask you, among these which one do you think is in your control? Is it events, action, or thoughts? Almost everyone tells me it's our actions and thoughts that are within our control. Let's delve deeper.

How are thoughts in your control? You may say "I choose which thoughts I want to entertain"—negative thoughts or positive thoughts. In this case "choosing" is an action, meaning action is within our control. We cannot control our thoughts because they are free flowing. But we can decide to reject or accept certain thoughts when they flow into our minds. When we do this, deciding becomes an action. We may not be able to stop all of the thoughts that are flowing through our minds, but we can certainly channel the ones that are the most beneficial in the right direction.

So when you think about "EAT," realize that it is only *action* that is within our control. Events come and go, and you have no control over them. Thoughts are free flowing, and you have no control over them. But you can choose and decide your response, so action is completely within your control. Let's understand this deeper with few examples that apply the EAT strategy here.

Case 1: It's Friday evening and you're excited to leave town for your friend's 40th birthday party. You get an email from your boss about a presentation due Monday morning.

Event: A sudden demand from your boss comes in an email about the presentation on Monday.

Thoughts: Why did she not give me more time? I can't do it in such a short notice. OR: Let me email her to request another deadline. What's the best I can do in this situation?

Action: The type of thought you select is the first step before you actually take action. Each thought will bring with it its own energy.

Case 2: You have been working hard on a project for a client. You have to deliver a 3-day workshop to their accounts department. You just found out your project might be canceled due to significant budget cuts in the department.

Event: You just found out your project might be canceled due to significant budget cuts.

Thought: I wasted my time and money. Nothing goes well in my life. OR: What is the next best step for me. Can I help them boost their budget?

Action: The type of thought you select is the first step before you actually take action. Each thought will bring with it its own energy.

Case 3: You have been looking forward to a well-deserved promotion. A colleague got a promotion over you.

Event: A colleague got a promotion over you.

Thought: Whatever I do, I will always be stuck where I am. He is always in my way. OR: How can I prepare more next time? What could I have done better?

Action: The type of thought you select is the first step before you actually take action. Each thought will bring with it its own energy.

Do you see how EAT works in every situation? Whether you're right or not is irrelevant. A month from now, the memory of your event will fade away. What you will remember is your action. This is when regret walks into your life. When you feel regret over something you always tell yourself, "I wish" I hadn't or had done such and such a thing.

It boils down to actions—our karmas. We don't blame the event as much as we blame our own karmas. We regret our actions. What we don't realize is that our actions arise from and are influenced by our thoughts. So if we take care of the thoughts, then the actions will take care of themselves. You are in control of choosing your actions. There are five types of thoughts the mind generates:

1. Necessary thoughts: reflections about one's experiences, responsibilities, finance, career, and family.
2. Wasteful thoughts: worrying about the past and future, being anxious, and feeling doubt.
3. Positive thoughts: goodness, happiness, joy, and peace.
4. Negative thoughts: jealousy, hatred, anger, and regret.
5. Sattvic (or energetic and nourishing) thoughts: purity of heart, a sense of self-discipline, and forgiveness.

Every thought is self-created. You can create consciously or unconsciously. Many generate unconscious thoughts that they are not aware they are creating. If you can create negative thoughts, you can create positive thoughts too. You can create thought, and you can create action. People in their career are successful or failing depending on the thoughts they have created and chosen to take pride of place within their minds. Our thoughts are linked with our karma. Well-chosen thoughts constitute action.

So if you feel burnt out, stressed, and overwhelmed at work, it may have more to do with your thought-creation than the work itself. You are the creator of the garden of your mind. What you plant and nourish within will be manifested in your outer environment. Your clients, boss, peers, teams, and the economy do not create the thoughts in your mind. These people and things are purely external individuals, events, and behaviors. The mind is a meaning-making machine. It creates thoughts with a certain meaning for every event that happens in your career. That is why I tell people that some of our problems can be illusions. They are opportunities to some and problems to others. Our mindset must precede our skillset.

A good technique to help move away from these negative thoughts is a simple technique I call, "Replace Please." Minding the mind requires a replacement strategy. If you tell your mind not to worry or overthink about a particular person or event, then guess what? You are actually reminding your mind of that event or person and reinforcing it. Instead of pondering "Why did this happen to me," and getting caught in a cobweb of negativity, simply tell yourself, "Replace Please" and substitute positive reflection for negative worrying.

I learned that our mind only successfully holds one thought at a time, just as we can only feel one emotion at a time. In your clearest and healthiest state, you can either be happy or sad; you can't be both at the same time. Likewise, in your clearest and healthiest state, you can only think a positive or a negative thought at a time. When you think undesirable thoughts, say to yourself "Replace Please." As soon as you say these words, you become aware of the quality of the thought and you consciously replace it with an uplifting thought.

You will be astounded as to how quickly it changes your state of mind and energy level. Your mind can progress or regress. The quality of your results depends on the quality of your mind. I tell my clients to go beyond positive and negative thoughts. Cultivate a sattvic mind— meaning, one with pure thoughts. A sattvic mind gives you the ability to visualize well, think right, do well, and act in accordance with the laws of nature. It creates equilibrium, balance, harmony, purity, and clarity. Whenever confronted with a situation that leads to undesirable thoughts, tell yourself immediately, "Replace Please."

Buddha, Norman Vincent Peale, Gandhi, Albert Einstein, Marian Diamond, Alexa Canady, Oliver Sacks, Patricia Goldman-Rakic—all of this historical and present-day men and women leaders in science or religion recognized the power of mind. People talk about how the business world is in turmoil, and no one is able to do anything about it. What about the turmoil within you? The outer turmoil may not be in your control, but the inner turmoil sure is. In fact, the outer turmoil in the work environment is because of the inner turmoil.

The mind never stops thinking. It thinks too much. It is always filled with chatter. Most people don't give any thought to the quality of their thoughts. And until we take some time to silence the chatter, we cannot go within and get the answers we want. It is very difficult to control the ever-moving mind. However, through sincere practice and dispassionate detachment, it can be achieved.

As a child, I often heard my teachers tell stories about heaven and hell. My father once told me that heaven and hell is a state of mind. When the mind falls victim to worries and anxieties, when the mind is disturbed, when it creates undesirable thoughts, when it does any of these things, we create hell in our lives. But when the mind thinks sattvic (pure) thoughts, we can be happy and full of peace, and we experience heaven. Both are within us in our daily life and conduct. Our workplace is heaven and hell because of each of us. We have the power to make our workplace blissful or sorrowful. We create negative and positive work environments. Each one of us can become the ambassador of positive environments. And as are you, so is your environment.

It helps to detox the mind everyday with the following inner actions:

1. Meditate for success.
2. Listen to inspirational talks.
3. Hear and repeat affirmations that uplift your spirit.
4. Be grateful.
5. Empty your mind of worries before you sleep.
6. Take couple of deep breaths every hour.
7. Sleep well.

The truth is, you become what your mind is. The mind does not possess you; you possess your mind. Stability of mind means remaining the same in all circumstances and under all conditions. This means that our mind should be in a state of equilibrium: success and failure should be on the same level and neither state should impact upon you.

Stop right now and repeat this mantra to yourself:

I am the creator of my thoughts.

It is said that a ship doesn't sink because of the water around it; rather, it sinks because of the water that enters it. You do not drown because of the negativity around you; you asphyxiate because of the negativity that enters your mind. The choice is yours alone! Drown or float! Let your mind be an asset to you, not a liability. Remember that while nature is timeless, our own clocks are ticking and the more we reduce the turbulence of the mind, the more we will move toward success. When you keep moving toward your goals with speed and serenity, you become unstoppable.

KARMA 2

Draw Your Blueprint

A blueprint is what you create about your future. It is the story you tell yourself. The best resources, opportunities, and outer factors will do no good if your blueprint is not ready. To manifest your desired results, draw your blueprint.

After you finish reading this paragraph, take some time, close your eyes, and try this exercise. Take a few deep breaths and relax. Picture yourself. Do you see yourself with a prosperous mindset or a scarce mindset? Do you have an attitude of plenty or attitude of lack? In the next year, do you see yourself as financially stable or unstable? Do you see yourself flourishing and thriving, or struggling and straining? How would you want your professional life to be? What are some of the things you want to achieve in your professional life? What are some of the things people are saying about you? Complete picturing scene by scene, and take a few deep breaths and open your eyes.

The picture you saw is the blueprint you have created. It is a script you write before you play your role in your career. Each of us creates a different blueprint based on many elements both internal and external such as experience, knowledge, belief system, culture, regrets, guilt, and happiness. And each of us acts in accordance with our blueprint. Our blueprint may look like this: complete graduation, get a good job, work hard, earn money, and retire with a big 401k plan. Another person's blueprint may be complete graduation, get a job in a Fortune 500 company, work hard, reach the top position, and earn a fortune. Someone's blueprint may tell her to skip college, get into a business, and take up a part-time job to support business and make millions. Everyone around you has a blueprint. And everyone acts according to the blueprint they have created. That is why around you, you see people, whether they are your teams, clients, or boss, take different actions. Even if you and I feel the action is inappropriate, it is what their blueprint tells them to do.

Pause for a moment to check if you have created your blueprint? We all desire growth and success. Precisely creating a blueprint does the magic. Can you think about people you know who say they're going to do something and then they never complete the task? Whereas a few people do something inside their head that gets them to follow through. Extend your thinking to people whom when you meet you are amazed at what they achieved in a year and then other people who amaze you that they haven't moved toward their goals.

Now, what about people who are excited about progress while others are pulling themselves each day? Have few names here too? Often, we look at people and wonder why someone does not take actions or how someone can be so passionate about their work? The answer is deep rooted in their blueprint. Some have created a clear and enriched blueprint and some an ambiguous one. The quality of your blueprint will decide the quality of your karmas (actions). My point is that you will put in effort based upon your blueprint.

An article in the *Seattle Times* articulated how, 6 months before his assassination, Martin Luther King, Jr. spoke to a group of students at Barratt Junior High School in Philadelphia on October 26, 1967. He started his speech by asking a question: What is your life's blueprint? To me, a career's blueprint is what will determine where your professional life will go. Those who lead themselves can lead any business or team. Self-integration comes before team integration. You can design your success.

I have had the opportunity to meet amazing business professionals and corporate leaders globally. They all have the business plan, marketing plans, and financial plans ready. They know their product and service and have learned about their competitors in the industry. Rarely do I meet anyone who comes prepared with a professional blueprint.

And those who have one, I have seen them pulsing with vitality as if they are sure they will get there and the path is ready for them. They know what to do in the event of challenges and obstacles. Designing a blueprint is an important tool for deciding what you want to do with your professional life, what your aspirations are, and how you can achieve your goals under a specific time frame.

When a building is under construction, the first thing an architect does is design the blueprint that serves as a guide for all of people who are to build the building. Without a solid blueprint, the building is not well erected. Similarly, you are in the process of constructing your successful career. For this, you too need to design a blueprint that will serve as a guide for you to move ahead.

For this the first step is to know where you are in your journey. It gives you a "helicopter view" of your career so that you can bring things back into balance. It helps you consider each area of your career life and assess what's off balance. You get a clear visual representation of the way your career is currently, compared to the way you'd ideally like it to be. It's a reality check that I encourage all of my clients to go through.

In the journey to success, it is so easy for us to be pulled off course. I have met people who reach mid-career or retirement age, look around, and realize that they have not achieved what they wanted to. They got distracted and pulled off course in their journey. People tell me all about their plans for the future and about their career and goals. But it's all in their heads. Plans in the head turn into headaches soon. Until you clearly articulate them on paper, you will continue to lose your perspective. This is a leading cause for people to feel unfulfilled in their career life. One has to be proactive in today's workplace. Proactivity requires that you be organized. This predominantly includes your mindset. What you picture within is what is executed outside. Investing time in creating your blueprint for success has many benefits such as the following:

- Your blueprint is an app that takes you from destination A to destination B. Each of us has future plans. In this plan, everything looks perfect. But when the rubber hits the road, things may go the unplanned way. During this phase many get frustrated, and they give up. People lose their passion, their confidence, their desire, and their happiness. Obstacles and roadblocks detour us on the way to success or even prevent us from getting there. Maybe you're getting that lost feeling right now in your professional life or in your business. We all get off track at some point. What is important is to get back on the road as quickly as possible. Navigating your way from your current location to your desired location is crucial. Whatever is your goal, then your blueprint will take you there. It is like a GPS (global positioning system), which keeps you on track, and when you get lost or stuck it shows you your direction based on the destination you feed it.

- Your blueprint gets you unstuck. Whichever phase of your career within which you are struggling, whether finding a job, moving ahead on the corporate ladder, starting or expanding a business, designing a blueprint gives you complete clarity. It shows you step by step how to get unstuck and progress ahead.

- It helps you get back on track when you detour. Work is hectic and pulls us in all different directions. And before you know it, you find yourselves on a road you never intended to take. When you take that wrong turn or stop along the curb, your blueprint helps you get back on track. It provides the direction needed to overcome obstacles and keep moving forward.

- Your blueprint gives you more control. In the game of soccer, the best players do not let the ball dictate their game and move. Similarly, in the game of career, do not let circumstances dictate you. We all know that obstacles and challenges will meet us in our entire career life. So why not be prepared to welcome them? A career blueprint helps you take control of your career and whenever you have more control, the less the stress.

- Your blueprint is the story you create. If you knew that you are the producer, director, and creator of your movie, what type of script would you write? Blueprint is the story you create. You can choose to create a story that is profitable or unprofitable.

- It relieves you of stress. Whenever you deviate from your plan, things are harder. Sometimes unknowingly we take up more than we should, creating stress. Blueprint helps you stay away from these situations. Success is all about progress. Your blueprint helps you move ahead by taking appropriate actions daily.
- Your blueprint helps you move forward. Success and growth gets challenging when you are scrambling for opportunities. It makes you feel lonely, and the journey seems tiring. Blueprint helps you to look forward toward your goals. It gives you hope. And as Thomas Carlyle rightly said, "he who has health, has hope; and he who has hope, has everything."
- Your blueprint helps you to finish strong. I have met numerous leaders and business owners who give up halfway in the journey, and this could be for a myriad of reasons. Whatever the reasons, a clear blueprint helps you to finish what you started.

Personally, I started to create my blueprint years back when I heard a story about John Stephen Akhwari in my business management class. I don't recollect everything what I heard about him. But I vividly remember few nuggets. I remember the teacher telling us that Akhwari didn't win a medal. In fact, he came nowhere near because of the injuries he faced during the race. Yet after receiving the medical treatment, he returned back on the track. He was asked why he'd carried on, and his response has gone down in sporting history. "My county did not send me 5,000 miles to start the race," he said. "They sent me 5,000 miles to finish the race." The word finish stayed with me. Have you ever observed that around you there are people who will always finish what they start? While others start with great enthusiasm but don't finish it. Finishing is harder than starting. It happened with me too, many times while studying my business management course. It was easy to start a project, but finishing it was another story in itself. In fact, even most parents support their children to start off on something, but very few encourage them to finish what they started. Extracurricular classes are full of children who aspire to become a pianist, a singer, a karate champion, a chess master, a mathematician, and more. Yet, when you check how many truly passed each level of the class and finished the course, the numbers are amazing. Only a couple out of thousands finish what they started. It's easy to dream. There is a Chinese story told of a man called Leyangtsi. His wife was very angelic and virtuous, who was loved and respected dearly by the husband. Once Leyangtsi went to a distant place to study classics with a talented teacher, leaving his wife home alone. One day, his wife was weaving on the loom, when Leyangtsi entered. At his coming, the wife seemed to be worried, and she at once asked the reason why he came back so soon. The husband explained how he missed her. The wife got angry with what the husband did. Advising her husband to have fortitude and not be too indulged in the love, the wife took up a pair of scissors and cut down what she had woven on the loom which made Leyangtsi very puzzled. His wife declared, "If something is stopped halfway, it is just like the cut cloth on the loom. The cloth will only be useful if finished. But now, it has been nothing but a mess, and so it is with your study."

Leyangtsi was greatly moved by his wife. He left home resolutely and went on with his study. He didn't return home to see his beloved wife until gaining great achievements.

Do you like Leyangtsi start off well but end up coming back halfway? If you want to finish strong, if you want to experience what it feels like to reach to your destination, then it is imperative to keep moving ahead without giving up halfway. Think about your goals. Do you want to hit a million dollars in sales? Do you want to grow your team? Do you want to speak at an industry conference? It is possible to achieve your goals when you have designed your blueprint. As the old saying goes, "failure to plan is planning to fail." If you want to end each year strong you need a plan to get you there. A plan for your leadership, a plan that will help you to never give up, a plan that will bring you back on track, a plan that will help you succeed.

Whatever you design on this blueprint is what comes into reality sooner or later. Your wishes come true, sooner or later. You must be careful what you design in your blueprint because you get what you wish for. This blueprint is the story you tell yourself that soon manifests itself in the form of reality. Whether you go for a meeting, talk on the phone with your boss, work on a project, motivate your staff, work on your growth, or do your routine work, remember that the blueprint you create around it is of utmost importance.

Not long ago I met Monica, a business owner. She was successful in stabilizing and to some extent growing her business. One of the major problems she was confronting was that her staff members weren't able to connect well with her. Her people avoided her, her management team was frustrated under her leadership, and there was colossal staff turnover every few months. She herself was going through stress and health problems because of these issues.

During our frequent meetings and conversations, I got to understand her blueprint. She had created a blueprint that was full of fear of her business getting into a loss and bankruptcy. This blueprint drove her to engage in karmas like distrusting her people, micromanagement, arguing to put her point across, anger, stress, no appreciation for staff, less bonus, and many more problems. Slowly her business incurred a loss. She often pondered over why her hard work and sleepless nights weren't paying off. She failed to understand that she acted based on what she created in her blueprint. Our blueprint is responsible for our actions.

No one from outside has the power to be the creator of your blueprint. Take this simple example. Most of the days the newspaper bleeds with news about downsizing, bankruptcy, unemployment, and economic slowdown. If you read in the paper that 35 percent of businesses are going bankrupt, does this sound an alarm? Do your thoughts go into red flag zone, making you think of the worse? Soon you begin to worry about your job or business. This is where the distraction sets it and drifts you away from your plan. Because of the worry you take actions, which you never intended to. But when you slow down your thoughts and think of who created this thought for you.

Was the news responsible for your misfortune? Not really! The report simply mentioned 35 percent of businesses going bankrupt, and that means 65 percent are still thriving. However, you chose to build your story around the thought that 35 percent are out of business and you saw yourself among that percentage. Your actions, results, and thoughts changed. The story you created blocked your thinking, steered it in the direction you never wanted to go, drained you out, reduced your potential, and made you take actions that delivered poor results. This is why a blueprint is of utmost importance. A career life is full of peaks and valleys. To not let the peaks get too high and the valleys too low, a blueprint is needed. It gives you a clear picture of where you want to go and what exactly to wish for.

Now, what if you have created an ambiguous blueprint? Many of us then try to destroy it in an attempt to create a positive one. Often, we still find ourselves back again in the unambiguous blueprint cycle. The main reason for this is that as humans, we hate to ruin our creation. Destroying is an action that depletes our energy. We love and feel comfortable with our creation. The blueprint you create is something that flows from your heart. It's your imagination. The ambiguousness is because of what's within you. So as hard as you may try, you aren't really successful in destroying it.

However, as humans, we like to create and recreate. So just as you created a negative story, recreate a positive story and send it out to the universe. Create and recreate based on your desired outcome. Never try to destroy your or anyone's blueprint, however shaky it may appear. You are in charge of your growth and success. Whenever you feel happy, it is because your conditions at work are matching your blueprint and whenever you are sad it is because your conditions at work are not by your blueprint. So, you have an option. Either enrich your blueprint or enrich your strategies and action. Because if you don't design your blueprint for success, chances you'll fall into someone else's blueprint, and there wouldn't be much planned in there for you. If you want to re-create your blueprint in the most effective way, a golden rule is to have "Outcome Clarity."

Most of us know what we want, but it isn't with clarity. When I ask my clients what is it that they absolutely want here are few answers that I get:

- "I want to expand my business."
- "I want to become the senior manager in my company."
- "I want to increase my network."
- "I want more clients in my business."
- "I want to increase my boutique sales."

Now, you may say these are good outcomes. Yes, they are, but they aren't clear. See, if outcomes are not clear the journey to achieve it will also be ambiguous. This is why people get frustrated while achieving their goals. Outcome Clarity means you have articulated your outcome as specifically as you can. Let's take one outcome from the above, "I want to increase my network," and write it meticulously. "I want to make ten contacts per day on my LinkedIn page with HR professionals to build a connection for moving to a new company by the end of this year." Observe closely, an outcome drafted in this manner spells out many aspects.

1. What you want.
2. Why you want it.
3. By when you want it.
4. How you want it.

Once your blueprint is ready, you will lead your career by design and not by default. You have designed your success. Here is one simple way to design your blueprint.

To create your successful blueprint, you have to embrace the form of an AVATAR. This is an acronym that stands for the following:

- **Aspirations:** what is your goal?
- **Virtue:** what qualities will you develop to achieve your goals?

- **Action:** what are some of the actions you will take to achieve your goals?
- **Time:** what is the time frame for you to achieve your goals?
- **Accountability:** how will you hold yourself accountable?
- **Reality:** where are you currently in achieving your goals?

A great deal of stress in work–life occurs because we don't spend enough time nurturing our self for the roles that are most important to us. The results you get in your career life are based on what you create within your mind in your blueprint. No one has the responsibility for your failure or success except you. It is not your boss, peers, family, or circumstances. It is only you. So, when you know this now, would it not be a great idea to start to create your success today?

KARMA 3

Shape Your Success

Is there a formula for success? Maybe. But for now, picture yourself driving a car and you have reached a crossroad with two potential paths to take. One road is familiar to you. You've traveled it more than often. It feels comfortable and gets you the same results. The second road is not traveled, a path that you've wanted to take but never traveled. It's a path of unknowns, and you don't know the results you will get. It requires you to take the risk and leave your comfort zone.

The car is your professional life in which you are the driver. One road is fueled by recurring results. The other is driven by new unknown results. Which road would you most like to drive your professional car on? Be aware and recognize the patterns in your career. Patterns are a curious blend of your karma and thought. We are followers of our own patterns.

Your success is a matter of two pattern types. One set of patterns leads to the same results that you've always wanted. Most of us have become complacent driving and traveling the known path. This is one of the biggest reasons why there is a gap between where we are and where we would wish to be. Repeating the same actions will get you the same results. Many people are stuck where they are in their professional lives because they are repeating their actions over and over again getting them the same results. Nothing will change outwardly unless something changes within. If outer events were responsible for your failures, no one should have been successful on this planet Earth.

The fact is a small group of people is successful and is achieving their goals consistently.

So, is there a formula to success? Yes, there is. The formula is hidden in your daily patterns. Patterns are your daily habits that either are or aren't serving you. Business owners get almost the same percentage of growth every year, individuals in the corporate world aspire for growth and get stuck in the same role for years, and business owners scramble for opportunism every year. All these create a feeling of frustration, and we land up blaming economy, government, management, and everyone and everything we can point a finger to except our own self. We make these patterns unconsciously and slowly become habituated with that. Others too, get familiar with our patterns. In my experience, I have noticed two types of patterns that govern our success process. They are the thought pattern and action pattern. Both are deeply interconnected in a way where one follows the other.

Thought Pattern

Generally, we create roughly 50,000–60,000 thoughts, so we need to be aware of the quality of our thoughts. Negative thought patterns compound extremely fast, whereas positive thought patterns are slow and do not need excessive build up. The way we think influences our action.

In one case, a husband and wife owned an advertising business. In the seventh year, their business should have been growing exponentially. But it was just the opposite. Their business had slowed down. They hired me to help them sustain their business and grow progressively. During the pre-coaching, I got to know that the main reason for the business not progressing was because the husband worked with certain thought patterns like micromanagement is necessary, people will not work until they are instructed, people will work only with reward and punishments, he does not have to change as he is the boss, his people do not respect him, and many other problematic patterns.

These patterns may sound outdated, or something prevalent only in small businesses, but, trust me, they aren't.

In my work with Fortune 500 companies, too, I have observed similar patterns. A senior manager I coached on leadership felt stressed at work and stuck in the same role for 6 years. He too had certain thought patterns, like, "people cannot be trusted to work on their own," "I must oversee all the work my team does," "I must do more work than others," "I must help my team in everything they do." Yet another director I worked with had certain thought patterns like planning ahead, trusting his people, allowing and learning from mistakes, and coming early to work.

Thought pattern means you develop a habit of thinking in a particular way, using particular assumptions. Your career life is all about how you think. Unknowingly we are trapped in a thought pattern, which is detrimental to success. Negative thought patterns are somewhat along these lines: "Why am I not promoted?" "No one understands me." "Why doesn't my business grow?" "Why don't I make as much money as he?"

Those with a negative thought pattern look at issues and opinions as black or white without truly putting themselves on the other side of issues. They take things personally and are on a constant lookout for problems. Their views and opinions are on the extreme. They believe they have a license to mind read, which is why you see them conclude that someone is reacting negatively, and they don't bother to check this out. They anticipate that things will turn out badly. In contrast, positive thought patterns could be expressed as follows: "How can I improve this?" "What can I do to scale up business more?" Those with a positive thought pattern look at things with a calm state of mind, seeing different perspectives.

Albert Einstein said, "Without changing our pattern of thought, we will not be able to solve the problems we created with our current patterns of thought." This is so true. If you wish to create new results or solve an existing pattern, check your current thought pattern that got you into the undesirable situation. Our thought pattern is the root of our external patterns that the world gets the chance to identify.

Action Pattern

This means you develop a habit of acting or behaving in a particular way, because of your thoughts. Most of the time, the difference between people who make it and those who didn't is the action pattern. It is said that if you are willing to take the actions today that others won't take, then you will increase your chances of getting tomorrow what others might not get. What is your action pattern? Do you wait and wait for circumstances to change or do you take the necessary actions to move ahead? I once heard a story from my business management teacher at school. It was about a dog that was crying softly for more than an hour.

A neighbor who heard the sobbing asked the owner of the dog what had happened. The owner said it's nothing but his habit of complaining. An hour passed but the dog's crying continued. The neighbor again asked the owner what the matter was. The owner said that the place where the dog is sitting has a small nail, which is pricking him and hurting his leg. This confused the neighbor as she asked why the dog would not move away from the nail.

It turned out that the dog's pain was still bearable to him, and he would move out and change his position when the pain is too much for him to bear. For now, he was comfortable with the pain. Today when I think about this story, I feel we all too are like this dog. We complain of the work problems we have and have become comfortable with that pain. We aren't willing to take immediate action. We do nothing about it until it becomes unbearable. And when it does become unbearable, we are already in a painful state of mind. This is why you see all around you that people continue to work in conditions detrimental to them. I have met numerous leaders who are unhappy with their current job, but would not take the necessary actions to move out and at all times the reason had been fear of losing control or fear of losing comfort.

Take a look again at the success blueprint you created in Karma 1. Are your current thoughts and work patterns helping you achieve your blueprint outcome? Action patterns are also seen in other ways like, the time you wake up in the morning, what do you read, and your work routine. For many of us, our instincts tell us that we should choose certainty over uncertainty and comfort over any discomforts.

To develop a pattern conducive for success there is a process called ADAPT. ADAPT is an acronym that stands for adjusting your patterns to work alongside with your blueprint. ADAPT has five steps to it: Awareness, Disrupt, Activate, Practice, and Trigger.

1. **Awareness:** Recognizing your current pattern is the first step to ADAPT. Take a pause and reflect on what pattern works. Examples are waking up early, checking and replying to every email, working late night hours, micromanagement, planning ahead, trusting team, thinking negatively, or positively. Now take a look at the patterns you have written. What are your patterns doing to and for you? Are they taking you toward or further away from success? It is very crucial to recognize your pattern. It is only when you are aware of your pattern that you will do something to change it. Most of us, if we are getting the same results with no further progress, are operating in a negative pattern loop. Negative patterns lead to failure and disenchantment. And if we are getting the new results with progress, it means we are operating in a positive pattern loop. Positive patterns lead to achievement and greater fulfillment in life.

2. **Disrupt:** Routines are great for getting us out of bed in the morning and keeping the momentum alive. But that does not lead to growth, expansion, and new beginnings. A pattern disruption is a technique to change a particular thought, behavior, or situation.

3. **Activate:** This is where you substitute the poor-quality patterns with new enriched patterns quality. You build new pattern.

4. **Practice:** The new pattern must be followed through to help you achieve your desired outcome. Practicing the new pattern takes time and effort. It is a bit like comforting your mind: "Of course you're not a loser. You might not have bagged this deal, but you took all the actions. And remember how you bagged two clients

last month?" You don't want to be a person who says they will do many things and then don't follow through. You want to be someone whose action and words go hand in hand. Practice is the best way out. Don't get dejected if you keep going back to your old pattern. The next step will show you just how exactly to anchor yourself to the new pattern.

5. **Trigger:** Every time the old pattern shows up, which it will until you have erased it completely, remind yourself to switch to the new one. This is what a trigger is helpful for. A slight pinch, a change of position, a walk, drinking water, a stand and sit set of routine juts anything to remind you to get back on track.

Success Modeling

Patterns can either fill your work life with stress and frustration or passion and fulfillment. The choice is yours. It takes a while to ADAPT. Once done, you want to make sure people who are in frequency with your new pattern surround you. Now our day-to-day work lifestyle doesn't leave much room for making connections with people around whom we want to be surrounded. But there are simple ways of doing this.

Think of three leaders or people in the workforce you admire. What qualities of theirs do you admire them for? What talents of theirs would you like to adopt? Now if you are ready with these answers, there is a technique to follow to ensure you enrich your patterns regularly. It is called "Success Modeling." *Success Modeling* means observing the ways others achieve the results you desire. It is replicating excellence. This is the most underutilized technique for being successful. I learned this technique when I was closely working with a CEO in the childcare industry. He would often say to us, "Don't reinvent the wheel."

Successful people have already left numerous clues and footprints for us and are still doing so. They know what works and what doesn't. So, start to achieve your outcome by studying how someone else goes about it. You model them in their body language, speed of voice, volume, and even word choice. Focus on what this person does, what he does not do, what are their thought and action patterns. This will start to shape you the way you wanted to be. That is why it is important to know whom you admire and what about them you admire.

Success Modeling slowly transforms your poor-quality patterns to the new ones to help you get to your desired outcome with speed. It helps you improve your performance. As Confucius said, "I hear and I forget. I see and I remember. I do and I understand." When you practice Success Modeling yourself, you are actually doing what successful people do.

Patterns can either fill your work life with stress and frustration or passion and fulfillment. The choice is yours. Let me close this chapter with Robert Frost's apt poem, "The Road Not Taken":

Two roads diverged in a yellow wood,
And sorry I could not travel both
And be one traveler, long I stood
And looked down one as far as I could
To where it bent in the undergrowth;
Then took the other, as just as fair,
And having perhaps the better claim,
Because it was grassy and wanted wear;
Though as for that the passing there
Had worn them really about the same,
And both that morning equally lay
In leaves no step had trodden black.
Oh, I kept the first for another day!
Yet knowing how way leads on to way,
I doubted if I should ever come back.
I shall be telling this with a sigh
Somewhere ages and ages hence:
Two roads diverged in a wood, and I—
I took the one less traveled by,
And that has made all the difference.

KARMA 4

Design Your Today

Have you played soccer, or taken part in a swimming competition, or played any sport for that matter? If yes, then you know the value of every second. You know that the difference between the winner and the runner-up is merely a few seconds. Every second counts when you are in a game. Every day counts before you get to play the big game. Design your today to design your future. Your actions today will determine the next event in your life.

I know this firsthand because I had the opportunity to coach a young man who was obsessed about swimming. When I met him at the age of 18, he was a person who would eat, sleep, and swim. He had no interest in earning, and life was tough for him because he was deaf and mute. But he never considered this as a limitation. He secretly harbored the dream to one day swim in the Olympics. He wasn't from a very affluent family and often his father worked night shifts to support the family.

During my coaching sessions, I noticed that he had become habituated to wake up late and eat too much. But then he had a complete makeover when he got a chance to join his college team. Every day he would wake up at 4:30 AM to do his stretches. Then at 5 AM he would go to practice with his school team, and at 6 AM he would come back home to get ready for school. After school, he would finish his homework and again practice on his own from 6 PM to 7:30 PM. This was his routine every day. Sunshine or rain, winter or summer, tired or fresh, it was his routine every day. His everyday routine got him to move on to regional and now the state level.

I do not coach him anymore because his school has now provided a coach for him to reach the next level. But we are in constant communication, and I still share with him countless tips and suggestions to ensure that he never gives up and keeps rising to the next level. His everyday routine brought him to his present state. Let me ask you this, what is your everyday routine? Can you think of at least two routines you have every day to accomplish your future goals?

Most of us know what we want. We have our goals and passion. It all comes down to your everyday actions. What do you do every day? If you want to become the manager or CEO of a company, you want to increase your income, expand your business, master a sport, whatever it may be all that matters is what you do every day. Your countless number of days to reach your destination is made up of one important day—your today. Your today is a major part of your everyday. Your today will lead to your tomorrow. A today that is wasted will need extra efforts on your part to recover and make up for it tomorrow.

Worry, anxiety, anger, too much excitement over social media, doing other people's work, hanging out with negative people, procrastinating, solving the same problem again and again, answering emails at crucial work hours, multitasking, checking phone often in the midst of work, not planning, dwelling in the past, carrying mental baggage, waiting for that perfect time, gossiping, socializing too much—all of these are problems that waste your time. One of the most common I have come across is the habit of people waiting—waiting for that opportunity, day, or meeting to move ahead. Sadly, their wait is never over.

It once occurred to the owner of a huge company that he would never fail if he knew key things. He rationalized that he must always know the right time to begin everything, and who were the right people to listen to and to avoid. Above all, he thought that if he always knew what was the most important thing to do, he would never fail in anything he might undertake. He consulted many learned men, but all had different answers and no one's answer satisfied him. On advice of his daughter, he decided to consult a highly learned man who was widely renowned for his wisdom. When the owner approached this man, the pundit was digging the ground in front of his hut.

The owner went up to him and said: "I have come to you, to ask you to answer three questions," and then he repeated the questions to him. The pundit listened to the owner, but answered nothing and recommended digging. Then the owner started helping the pundit with digging. After a couple of hours, the owner repeated his questions. The pundit again gave no answer. Again, after some time the owner said, "I came to you, wise man, for an answer to my questions. If you can give me none, tell me so, and I will return home."

Just then they saw a bearded man come running out of the wood, holding his hands pressed against his stomach which was profusely bleeding. He fell fainting on the ground, moaning feebly. The owner and the pundit unfastened the man's clothing. There was a large wound in his stomach. The owner washed it as best he could and bandaged it with his handkerchief and with the pundit's towel. Meanwhile the sun had set, and it had become cool. So, the owner got tired from his walk and from the work he had done and fell asleep. When he awoke in the morning, he found the strange bearded man lying on the bed and gazing intently at him with shining eyes.

"Forgive me!" said the bearded man. "I do not know you, and have nothing to forgive you for," said the owner. "You do not know me, but I know you. I am that enemy of yours who swore to revenge himself on you, because you destroyed my brother's business. I knew you had gone alone to see the hermit, and I resolved to kill you on your way back. But the day passed and you did not return. So, I came out from my ambush to find you, and came upon your bodyguard, and they recognized me, and wounded me. I escaped from them, but should have bled to death had you not dressed my wound. I wished to kill you, and you have saved my life. Forgive me!"

The owner was very glad to have made peace with his enemy. The owner approached the pundit again and said, "For the last time, I pray you to answer my questions, wise man."

"You have already been answered!" said the pundit. "Do you not see?" replied the pundit. "If you had not helped me in digging the ground but had gone your way, that man would have attacked you, and you would have repented of not having stayed with me. So, the most important time was when you were digging the beds; and I was the most important man; and to do me good was your most important business. Afterwards, when that man ran to us, the most important time was when you were attending to him."

Remember then: there is only one time that is important—now! It is the most important time because it is the only time when we have any power. The most necessary person is the one with whom you are, for no man knows whether he will ever have dealings with anyone else: and the most important affair is to do that person good, because for that purpose alone are we sent to this life.

Many of us, like this business owner, would like to know the right time to begin everything; the right people to listen to, and, above all, what is the most important thing to do. Countless books and articles have been written on mindfulness and living in the present moment. Most of us are aware of the importance of being in the today, in the present moment. Yet how many of us can vouch that with the knowledge we have on this subject of present moment, we have succeeded in living in the now, at least most of the days? Our thoughts, like a playful child, crawl into various corners of past and future, making us excited or sad. We are unaware of when our thought and conversation drifts away to the past or future.

In my daily interactions with business owners and corporate leaders, I have observed that people find it impossible to stay grounded in the present day. Even though the present day is all we have, our conversations surround the past and future. We either lament over something we failed to achieve in the past, or dream and plan of things to get in the future. I frequently ask my clients three questions:

1. What are your big plans for today?
2. What are two things you want to accomplish today?
3. How do you plan to end your day today?

As simple as these questions sound, you will be amazed that answer is never with clarity. In fact, their talk about past and future were clearer. We all have hopes and aspirations. We must plan for our future. However, you cannot live your future. If you want to achieve your future goals, you should remain engaged constantly, in your moment-to-moment activities. Your daily routine sets the tone for your future. In my work as a coach, I spend a lot of time with my clients at their office. Their daily routine gives me a clear picture of whether they will be successful or not in achieving their goals. For you to achieve your career goals you must design your today. This reminds me of the Buddhist monk's sayings. Each day ask yourself:

- Who am I today?
- Where am I going to today?
- Why am I going there today?

By doing so, you are designing each day for the future. Success depends largely on what you do today. Have there been times when you knew about a promotion happening in your company? You know there are a few people in your department who will be promoted, but you are not aware if your name is in that list too. At night you were unable to sleep peacefully because you feared you might miss this opportunity, only to know in reality that your name was on the list.

Or has it ever happened that the next morning you were to have a meeting with a potential client and that night were you unable to sleep peacefully because you worried that the next day meeting will decide your business future only to know in reality that your meeting got rescheduled to a month later. Or have there been times when you were so excited for the next day because you knew that it was going to be the best day of your work as you are being awarded the manager of the year. That night where you were unable to sleep peacefully because you were dreaming of the future so much that the next day you will interact with the top management, only to know that a family emergency did not allow you to be present for the award.

In all of the above examples, losing sleep, worrying or having anxiety means lack of energy to think and act the next day. To design your future, you need a high positive energy in the present moment. Your energy cannot be divided into worry, anxiety, frustration, or too much excitement. So, what do we do about such old friends, worry, anxiety, your past and future, who overstay their welcome, eat away your time, and suck the energy you have? No doubt that looking over the past allows us to reflect and avoid repeating mistakes, and looking at the future allows us to dream big. But now, in the present moment, is when we need to take our actions. You have to ask your old friends to move on. You have to make sure they visit on occasions when you need a gentle reminder of the past or the future. You must ensure you do not make them too comfortable. What you accomplish each day is more important than what you accomplish tomorrow or in a year.

Each day you consciously have to build a routine that you follow. When you wake up in the morning, are you clear in your head as to how your day will be? Have you written down what you will do to achieve your goals? Now you can do this only if you have reflected the previous night about the day gone by. You see, every today is based on the foundation of yesterday and every tomorrow is based on the foundation of today. So, what you do today is important. Each day when you wake up, do you prepare yourself for success or failure? Each day do you eat healthy, think healthy, and work healthy? The choice you make today will determine your tomorrow. Your actions today will determine the next event in your life.

Every day you are moving closer or further away from success. I recollect my high school days when each day attendance was taken to check if you are present or absent. Only a certain amount of absence was allowed in one school year. There were groups of girls and boys who would come to class to mark themselves present and then on any pretext would leave the class. Officially they were present, but mentally and physically they were absent. Soon their grades were low, and they were struggling to make it to the next grade. The same is in our professional life.

You go to office or to the client meeting and mark yourself present each day. However, within few minutes or an hour you are mentally absent because you are either quarreling with your past or struggling to see a better future. In both cases, it depletes your energy, makes you unproductive for that time, lowers your action, and results are down. A great future demands great results in the today. So, whatever is your BIG goal, chunk it down to your today. Break that one big goal to every day single day's goals. This will help you to do the following:

- **Generate new energy:** As soon as you put your thoughts in the present moment you will observe how much new energy flows into you. This energy that was drained into past and future thoughts gets together in the form of new energy, which allows you to focus more. Focus will bring you more ideas, more positivity, and eventually lead to your success.
- **Grab opportunities:** While being in the present and keeping full focus on the task at hand, you get aware of things around you. This means you rarely miss opportunities that come your way. New opportunities mean more success.
- **Be worry free:** Because you are not fretting over the past nor are you stressed about the future, your mind becomes free of worry. You will not think of worst outcomes and automatically negativity will be away from you. A worry-free mind will release happiness and keep the mind relaxed, which will eventually show up in the form of good physical health and success.

No doubt we cannot and should not stop thinking completely about the past or planning for the future, however changing gears often to the past and future, allowing it to drain you down in sadness or excitement is harmful. Just for today, observe your conversation with your friends, peers, spouse, boss, and children. Are the conversations around past and future or are they about today? What about your thoughts? When you are alone do your thoughts sway into the past and future? Our past and future are not in our control, yet the mind shift gears into the past and future? It is because when we shift gears it reminds us of something that made or will make us happy or sad.

Maybe you have beautiful memories of the past, like you had the best team, great boss, thriving business, or an admirable job title. Even these pleasant memories will make you feel sad in the present moment because you will either miss them or desire them more in the future. You were successful yesterday, you had five clients yesterday, and you became the manager yesterday. Who are you today? You will become the future CEO of the company, and you will establish a thriving business. Who are you today? What are you doing today? Today, are you complaining, whining, sad, passionate, action oriented, smiling, happy, dejected, disturbed, or calm? What are you doing today, and what are the actions you are going to take today that will determine your next day? Today, there is a lot of stress in organizations. Stress is caused by being "here" but wanting to be "there."

Most of the time we blame people and situations for whatever bad happens in our life. And we love to take credit of whatever good happens. But if you just rewind your day or week, you will pleasantly discover that both bad and good situations that you think of have happened because of your actions yesterday to that particular problem or person.

We all have a past, and we all dream of the future. These are important parts of our life. How we use them is what matters most. Do you look at your past with a regret or rejoice? Learning lessons from the past, which you can apply in the present to glorify your future is the best way to deal with past thoughts. The more you carry the burden of yesterday, the heavier your today becomes. And if you are not ready to handle the present correctly, it will build an imperfect future. And results are always in the future! Living in the present is an essential necessity to master the art of career success. As the Buddha put it, "The secret of health for both mind and body is not to mourn for the past, not to worry about the future, and not to anticipate troubles, but to live in the present moment wisely and earnestly."

One of the ways I derived to help my clients get the best out of their present moment is called *Compartmentalization*. You organize your stuff on your desk and have separate compartments for books, pens, paper, and files, just as you compartmentalize computer files into folders. Similarly, to help yourself to get the best out of the present moment you must compartmentalize. It's about putting thoughts and emotions where they belong and not letting them get in the way of the rest of your day. You must compartmentalize your thoughts and emotions and your day.

Acknowledge your positive and negative emotions and thoughts the moment they arrive. Let them know you will get back to them. There's a time to reflect and think about things. There may be certain times of day when you have a greater ability to do this. Just as we prioritize our to-do list, you need to prioritize your thoughts and emotions. If the thought or emotion is important and required at this moment, try to get to it so that it does not nag you all day long.

This is something most of us are aware of and maybe even practicing. Compartmentalize your day so you can get the best out it. Divide the 24 h into "active" and "inactive" compartments. Whatever tasks are of utmost importance or the ones you want to accomplish but have been procrastinating should go into the active compartment. The most productive time is morning until lunch (around 1 PM). During this time enter the active compartment and focus on the task at hand. Since you have already compartmentalized your thoughts and emotions, no one will disturb you while you are in the active compartment. The inactive compartment is for all tasks that you can do without having to bother about their immediate results. Like eating, sleeping, replying to emails, and making next day agendas.

Learning how to compartmentalize means knowing how to manage yourself such that you still get to do what needs to get done. Instead of ignoring thoughts and emotions, you are setting aside time to reflect and deal with them. You will be amazed that within just a few weeks of practicing this art, your mind will be conditioned to act as per your commands. It will not disturb you at work and will be your best buddy, helping you succeed. Leadership through mind helps you navigate the career maze calmly in the present moment.

To fly high like a kite you must be light. Light without any burdens of past and future. Only then will you be able to fly high. All of us have a reservoir of energy within us. The problem is we have distributed some of this energy in the past and some in the future with very less remaining in the today. Pull all that energy to today, bring it in your now and enjoy the flow of this energy in your today. With this energy design your today, it will design your future. Don't split yourself in the past and future because both your past and future require energy too. We are filled with positive energy, an energy that will make us prosper. Feel the power of this moment and success will be yours. Career life passes by very quickly. Every moment is born and dies as soon as it happens. When you realize that every moment is precious and not to be taken for granted, that the moment gone would not come back, you will give your best in your present moment.

Designing a today gets overwhelming for many business owners and corporate leaders. This is mainly due to the fact that they have so many goals and projects planned out that it seems impossible to fit it in the today. Below are two techniques, which my clients and their teams have been practicing on regular basis. It is called A3 and C2.

A3 Means Awareness, Agenda, Action

Awareness: Before you retire for the day, reflect on the day that passed by. Be aware of the things you did and did not do.

Agenda: After being aware, now create your agenda for the next day. This is different from the to-do list. Below is the sample of how to make an accomplishable agenda.

Action: This is the most important step. This is where most people fall short. You must take actions based on your awareness of yesterday and your agenda. If there is a pressing issue or something else that requires your attention, you have to decide whether it can be let go or acted upon.

C2 Means Capture and Chunk

Capture: There are many ideas that flow into our heads all day. We have many plans for today as well as for our career. Capture is a process where you put down all the plans that are in your head on paper or your computer. Don't let them fizzle away from your mind.

Chunking means breaking down big goals into specifics like what, when, who, how, and why. This makes it very easy to take action steps toward the big goal.

KARMA 5

Build Your Legacy

My work takes me places and oftentimes it's by air. During one of my flights to Chicago, the air hostess ensured that everyone was comfortable right before takeoff. As she came toward me, she said, "Ma'am, please fasten your seat belt. We will take off shortly and it will be a smooth one."

"What about the landing?" I asked her in humor. She smiled. For some time, my life has been all about takeoff and landing in visiting corporations to facilitate trainings and workshops on Leadership Through Mind. Your career too is about the takeoff and landing. In this journey, our takeoff, which is the start of our career, is beyond our control. We don't know the first company we will be hired by, the starting salary we will receive, the city, or country we will be in, the way business will commence, or who will be the first client. The first job or the first client we get is the takeoff.

The landing, which is the end of our career, is also beyond our control. You do not know which company you will end your career with, how much business will scale up, what salary, and what grade will you leave at. During this journey, the turbulences you face too are beyond your control. Turbulences such as budget problems, economy, stock market, corporate issues, people problems, client issues, downsizing are beyond your control. However, in this journey, there is one thing you have in your control. The choices you make during the journey.

The dates in your career, from takeoff to landing, are not important. What matters most is the dash in between those years. For this dash speaks volumes about all the times you were at work and those with whom you associated knew the meaning of that little dash. It speaks about the choices you made and the lives you impacted at work. It speaks about how you treated people and communicated with them. It speaks about the relations you built with people around. It speaks about your influence and commitment. Let me ask you this, if you knew today that it is your last working day, when you look back at all the years, what type of legacy will you leave behind? What will your people remember you for?

Think of five qualities that you would like your team to remember you for...Now ask yourself, "Do I already possess these qualities?" If not, it's time to build on them. Each of us has limited number of days in the workforce. None of us know when is the day of exit from the business and corporate world. Usually people think of the exit as a day of retirement. But in a world of disruptions and change, exit can take place any day. Today you are here working in a company soon you might get a lucrative offer and may be headed within the next 15 days to a new company.

Right now, you are doing well in your career, and tomorrow your name might be in the layoff list. Today your clients are doing business with you, and tomorrow they might terminate the contract. Who knows what the next moment or future is going to bring.

"Teach us to number our days that we may gain a heart of wisdom," says the singer in Psalm 90:12 of the Bible. It is important to know that learning to number your days at work is essential in order to do the best we can. None of us knows how much time we have left in our careers. None know how the separation from the professional life will take place. We do not have control over these components. But one thing is guaranteed: our days in our professional life are numbered. Are you prepared? Another thing that is for sure is that each of us will leave a legacy behind that is inevitable. What type of legacy you choose to leave behind is completely in your control. Reflect on what gift you want to leave behind.

Having coached people in different roles, from individual contributors to CEOs and business owners, I came to realize that most of the time one thinks of forging a legacy when they reach a certain position, specifically CEO positions, or when they are nearing retirement. My question is how long would you wait before you start to work on designing your legacy? How do you know if you will reach that position or achieve the targets in your current company? What if tomorrow you move to another company for better prospects? What if you don't wake up in the morning to be on your feet and get to work?

In my visit to an attorney's firm to conduct a leadership breakthrough session, I got to hear of James. James was one of the finest attorneys on that firm. I got to know that his skills and expertise were exceptional. His clients loved him for his honesty, judgment, communication, and people skills. James made it a point to take care of his health with proper diet and exercise. His team appreciated how he never shook hands with worry and stress. One morning James did not come to work. On investigating his boss got to know that when James woke up in the morning his body was paralyzed below the waist. He was hospitalized and doctors detected it was a rare disease called Guillain-Barré syndrome (GBS), a disorder in which your body's immune system attacks your nerves.

James hasn't been able to get back to work, but his people remember him for his honesty, people skills, worry free, and healthy life. He has left behind a legacy of investing in people and encouraging people to pass on everything they learn from one another. None of us know when there will be a separation from the career life. Each of us will leave a legacy, but what kind of legacy is an important question to reflect on? What if the people you work with move to other job or country? What will they remember about you? No one knows when the time of departure will arrive and you have to pack up and move on.

And later when we look back, we see there are conflicts yet to be resolved, there are relations still to be mended, and there are words of appreciation yet to be delivered. There are moments of compassion still to be revived. All the years you work hard, earn money, progress, and when it's time to pack up and move on, all that you take with you is regret, guilt and disappointments buried under the happiness of progress, which seems insignificant at the time of leaving.

During one of my sessions, I met Mathew, a senior manager in a Fortune 500 company. He was 10 years from retirement. After my session on "Unstoppable Leadership," Mathew came up to me and said, "Can I speak to you for a couple of minutes?" We decided to talk over a cup of coffee in the company cafeteria. Mathew said to me, "I have worked all my life as an IT engineer. Life went by so quickly with daily meetings, international travel, progressing ahead, global teams, earning for the family that when I look back, I feel I haven't done anything significant where I will be remembered by my people at work. This is making me feel dejected because I am nearing retirement." He took a deep breath. I could sense his feeling of despondency.

We spoke about what he would be remembered for when it's time to pack up and move on. That night I thought about what Mathew said that he hadn't done anything "significant" where his people at work would remember him. The word significant caught my attention more than anything. Most of us when we think of legacy, we think of leaving behind something big or doing something significant to be remembered. It is not your fault if you think like this because in the business world today, numbers make success. The number of copies a book sells, how much turnover the company has, how much do you earn, how much does your business generate. So, everyone is in a race to do something significant to be remembered.

In an attempt to accomplish these numbers and goals, we miss the daily opportunity to design a legacy. After the birth of my child, I decided to take a break from the corporate world for a couple of years. I submitted my resignation, and my team bid me a farewell in an emotional way and saying I would be missed a lot. Well now that is something that everyone says when you leave so I did not take it too seriously.

A couple of months later when I was settling in America, I learned from my family and a few peers that after I left many from my team also resigned. My parents shared with me that even after two years of my leaving, when my colleagues and management team meet my family, they talk highly about what I did for the people in the company. When I look back at this incident, I fail to understand what significant thing I did that left a positive legacy for which I am remembered even years after exiting the company.

Nothing significant, except my daily interactions with people and day-to-day work. Mother Teresa said it best, "There are no great acts, only small acts done with great love." When I look back, I understand now that legacy is built in your everyday actions, your karmas. Who knew that within a month I would resign, pack up, and move on? But what I did each day while working for is what built up my coworkers' perception of me.

If you haven't yet consciously designed your legacy, it's time to start to build your legacy *today*. Today you have the opportunity. Today you have the time. Today you are alive. Today you are here. Today and each day design your legacy. It is not about doing something significant, it is about the daily acts that build it up. While many corporate and business leaders I work with have their company mission and vision statement clearly drafted, they do not have their professional legacy statement clearly drafted.

A legacy statement helps you to express what you would like to be remembered for when it's time to pack up and move on. As soon as you design your legacy statement, you will feel the urge to work toward achieving it. Having gone through this awareness of designing your legacy, you will feel that you've given yourself a direction and that you are leaving behind something worthwhile. Whenever it's time to pack up and move on, you would feel a sense of fulfillment. Having coached several professionals on how to build a solid and strong legacy, I hear them share that if tomorrow they have to pack up and move on, they will not have regrets or guilt. They have a sense of contentment that whenever they will be remembered, it will be for a legacy they chose to design. What are the small acts that you do every day? It is these small acts that will build a big legacy. Every person in your company must design their legacy starting *today*. Each of us plays an important role in passing the baton to more capable hands.

Today's business world is challenging and complex and simply being highly effective isn't enough. To thrive, innovate, excel, and lead, we need to reach beyond effectiveness. Research shows that most people are not thriving, fulfilled, or happy at their workplace. If we continue in this state, what type of legacy will we leave behind? Everyday there are opportunities for people in all areas of business to leave a legacy.

Reflect on what it is you want to create in your life and, more importantly, what gift you wish to leave the world when you are no longer here. To be effective and highly productive in your daily job, you must first create the legacy you want to leave behind. This helps you to know what are some qualities you wish to leave behind, which implies these are the same qualities you want to imbibe in yourself first.

Do you love what you do? Do you wake up thinking about how much you enjoy it? Do you go to bed at night thinking about how you're going to do it better tomorrow? These are a few questions I ask participants during my weekend seminar as I speak to them about their leadership. How do you know if you genuinely love your work? As a leader and business owner, if you truly love your job you will continuously find opportunities to make the life of your people better each day. Ask yourself these few questions:

- Whom did I connect with today?
- Who may need a little TLC (tender loving care) today?
- Whom did I support this week?
- Who am I grateful to today?
- How can I make someone feel special today?

To close this chapter, I am going to ask you to sit in solitude for a couple of minutes to complete this exercise. Don't read further chapters until you have honestly worked on this piece.

Step 1: Imagine that you have retired today from this career life. Write a farewell speech that you would like to have read at your last working day. Add in the qualities you would like to be remembered for by your people.

Step 2: What are five action steps you will take today onwards that helps you match the qualities you have written in your farewell speech?

With loads of work upon us, it would be easy to let the light of compassion, hope, and kindness become dim from our leadership traits. But as Martin Luther King, Jr. said, "Darkness cannot drive out darkness; only light can do that. Hate cannot drive out hate; only love can do that." How are you showing compassion and care at work? I can almost assure you, your legacy will be the most important thing you will be remembered for by your people. Take care of the dash and start to make little changes to design a memorable legacy.

KARMA 6

Activate the Success Within

How's the weather where you are? I am not asking about the kind of weather that you experience when you walk outdoors, but the weather within you. You can't control the weather outdoors, but you can influence the climate within you to bring out the best in yourself. Our entire life at work involves changing the environment. Most of the time we fail. Work pressures like deadlines and relationships with colleagues make us chronically tense and stressed. You can't control the weather outdoors, but as a leader, you can influence the weather within yourself.

Earlier this year, I had a conversation with a business owner. He said, "When I enter the office in the morning, I can feel the tension. People barely acknowledge each other." Over the years, I've had similar conversations with a number of people in different industries and businesses of all sizes. It's easy to blame each other and say, "If she would communicate better, things would improve," or "If the teams stopped being negative, our office environment would be better."

While I was working in a mid-sized advertising agency, I was fortunate to be coached by a senior manager. Once we were conducting interviews with two candidates shortlisted for an ad designer position. The first candidate had all the skills we were looking for at our ad agency. As we concluded his interview, this candidate asked my manager about the work environment at the agency. My manager responded by asking him, "How was the work environment in your previous job?"

"Oh, it was so toxic," the candidate said, "There was lack of transparency, inconsistent policies, negativity, my boss lacked leadership skills, and my colleagues were unprofessional. But the pay was good and we had enough opportunities for trainings." My manager thought for a while and said, "In that case you will not be comfortable here as this place is a replica of what you just said." The candidate thanked him for letting him know this and left.

Then we spoke with our second candidate. I did not find his skills as strong as the first candidate. As we concluded his interview, he too asked us about the work environment. To this my manager responded by asking him, "How was the work environment in your previous job?" The candidate said smilingly, 'Oh, it was awesome. My boss was a great leader and mentor, and my colleagues were professional. There were gossipers, but we handled it. Communication wasn't the best, yet we were all kept within the loop, and the mood within the company was positive. I loved where I worked and it is because of pay that I am looking for a change."

My manager thought for a while and said, "In that case you will be comfortable here as this place is a replica of what you just said." The candidate thanked him for letting him know this and left. When examining the choice, my manager decided to select the second candidate.

"What? Are you wondering why I selected the second candidate despite the first candidate's skills on his résumé?" asked my manager, smiling at my confused facial expression. "Or are you thinking about how can the same place be said as good to one candidate and bad to another?"

He read my mind exactly. "You take yourself with you everywhere. Your behavior is a result of belief. We act on what we believe." My manager meant that mindset always precedes skill set. Then he went on to say the following: "The first candidate views his workplace as toxic and he will carry that attitude and belief with him here too. He is looking for a change to find the perfect workplace. The second candidate views his workplace as positive in spite of things being imperfect. He will carry that attitude and belief with him here too. We need that and as with skills, he will develop them soon. He will be successful outside because he is successful within. Remember, you take yourself with you everywhere," he concluded.

What a thought. You take yourself with you everywhere. That means if you feel successful, your success follows you everywhere. If you feel like a failure, you take failure with you everywhere. Did I not tell you in the introduction that success does follow you and you needn't pursue it? If you feel negative, you carry negativity with you to your workplace and vice versa. Wow. Think about it. What are you carrying with you daily to your workplace? Success or failure, positivity or negativity, abundance or lack, tension or serenity? Before we go deeper into this topic, take a moment and reflect on the following questions:

- How do you describe your current weather (meaning, your internal feelings and emotions)?
- What do you generally do when such feelings surface?
- Which feelings do you want to generate every day?
- In one word, how would you like to feel each day?

Now let's go deeper. If I were to ask you, "What is the meaning of success" I am sure you will have your own definition. However, the bottom line is that whatever we do, whichever industry within which we work, whatever role we play, we want to be successful. Have you ever met anyone who wants to fail in what they do? Success is what we wish for financially, professionally, and personally. However, few are achieving it.

Now most of us may agree that success is temporary. It's a hat that changes heads often. And in this era, are we working hard each day, losing peace of mind for something temporary? What if you didn't get success after all your hard work? What if for five years you did everything possible to get to the director's position only to find out your colleague got it? What if your business is thriving and your spouse's company has relocated him to another city where you would need to restart business?

Most people give up on pursuing success when tough and challenging situations attack us at work. Many believe success has a limited scope that is not achievable by everyone. Some feel it does not even exist. The main reason for this belief is because a majority of us look for success outwardly. We believe success in our career is because of the economy, peers, or our boss. Since we are pursuing success, we become like that child whose toy breaks and the child cries again for another one, and when that breaks, he cries again for another one. When the child does not get it, he is sad. When we pursue success, we feel sad when we don't get it.

If you are looking for success, it should be a success that is unbreakable and permanent. It cannot be something you are looking from outside of yourself. You cannot be dependent on external factors. You cannot wait for success to happen. I have heard many people tell me, "I will feel successful when I achieve my goals," or "I will feel successful if I become a director," or "I will feel successful if I get 25 clients this year." Most of us have been conditioned to think that success is something that will happen in the future. That is the reason we concentrate so much on results in a way that increases our stress and anxiety. Success is within you, and you do not have to wait until you reach a certain age, goal, or accomplishment.

Often our success is dependent on people, performance, goals, and money. We tend to work believing the equation:

I achieve and that is why I am successful.

When I am invited to talk about the concept of "Success Is Within" to high school students, I usually ask them as a simple question, "Do you feel you are successful today?" Most of them answer, "NO." I ask them to give me some reasons why they feel they are not successful. They say they don't have power and control yet, but once they achieve their dream, they can proudly say they are successful. They are following the equation, "I achieve and that is why I am successful."

When I tell them to write down the things they have achieved until today from the time they started their kindergarten years, they all have a long list. I probe them further, asking, "You all have a long list of your achievements, but why do you not feel successful?" The students are agile in their response. "We are looking to achieve the American Dream." Ah, I get it; they want to achieve that big car, house, business, position, and salary. This means that their achievement level has changed. Every time achievement level changes, we feel that we are not successful.

Look around you at your workplace and at yourself too. Do you see yourself or your people following the equation, "I achieve and that is why I am successful?" Now, you may question what's wrong with this equation? Do you feel successful when you perform well, exceed targets, achieve goals, and make more money? Yes, sadly, this is the culture within which we work today: achievement equates success. Doing more is considered successful.

Think about it: is achievement making you genuinely feel successful? What if you don't achieve? Now how do you feel? Like a failure? And until you achieve, you continue working with the feeling of failure. When you continue your work with this feeling, your energy depletes and your state of mind is disturbed. All these influence your karmas and results. Limited or reduced results make you feel like a failure. The entire cycle keeps getting you the same results every time.

During this time, you feel low and dejected, your state of mind is disturbed, and your energy is low. When the winds of challenge blow and obstacles try to stop you, you break down further. What is the quality of your emotion now? Will it allow you to think positive and make a beneficial decision? It is like saying if your immune system is weak and a virus is going around, it's easier for the virus to attack you and spread through your system faster and weaken you further.

Personally, in my interaction with corporate leaders and business owners, I have witnessed how they let external circumstances alter their belief about success. The traditional idea of success is linked to externals: you get this type of success when you make enough cash and secure the right amount of fame and get the right houses and receive the big title. This is why most of us experience a seesaw-like feeling in our careers where at times, we feel happy and excited, and at other times, we feel unhappy and stressed. There are days we feel successful and days where we feel unsuccessful. We have conditioned ourselves to believe that achievement is equal to success. Today most corporates and businesses are seeing stressed employees, unhappiness and negativity, demotivation, high staff turnover, limited results, and low productivity. It's not rocket science to know how to get back happiness, motivation, passion, and serenity in your business world. Simply switch the equation:

I am successful and that is why I achieve.

This equation changes your entire perspective. There is a vast difference in your attitude, energy, state of mind, and karmas as soon as you say to yourself that I am successful that is why I achieve. This means you have immense success within you. You achieve whatever you put your mind and heart wishes to achieve. You carry unlimited success with you each day. Success is within you. It is your self-belief that can do wonders. When you believe from within that you are successful it starts to change your energy.

Let me tell you the story of Ben Hogan, a prize-winning golfer. The 1950 U.S. Open was his first tournament after his car crashed head first into a bus. It was a crash that, by all logic, should have killed him. It almost certainly would have killed him, but it seems just before impact Ben Hogan leaned over to protect his wife, Valerie, and this move not only saved her life, but his own. He fractured his collarbone, pelvis, ankle, and rib, and doctors proclaimed his golf career over. Sixteen months later, Hogan was at Merion for the U.S. Open.

If you carry success within you, you can achieve whatever you want wherever you are. Your outer success is dependent on your inner success. None of us know what's next in our careers. Nor should you worry about it because you are successful within. Embrace the power within you because it truly makes you achieve. How do I know that, you ask? Read through the autobiographies of people like Ben Hogan who have made it big, and you will find out how they made the most of the toughest of circumstances, turning rock bottom into a slingshot to new heights.

In Matthew 21:21, the Bible tells us that if you have faith and do not doubt, not only can you do what was done to the fig tree, but also you can say to this mountain, "Go, throw yourself into the sea, and it will be done." This is because success is within you, within me, and within each of us. The only difference is that those who make it big use this power to the fullest. They do not chase success because they are very sure that they are successful within and can achieve their goals.

As the world was celebrating and welcoming the New Year in 2000, I remember seeing a news report about Amitabh Bachchan, an Indian Bollywood megastar, who was facing one of the toughest phases of his life. Despite his successes, he had faced near-death experience and many struggles throughout his career. At the age of 57, he had made more than enough money, had many luxuries, and was on the verge of retiring. But he faced bankruptcy. But every time life gave him a blow, he was resilient. Today he is back in the industry, out of debt, and seen in Hollywood films like *The Great Gatsby* alongside actors like Leonardo DiCaprio. Bachchan is also named "Actor of the Millennium" in a BBC news poll. He is again victorious. This happens only when you know with full conviction that immense success is within you.

Success needs to be built from the inside-out and not from the outside-in. Nick Vujicic, Arunima Sinha, Bethany Hamilton, Karoly Tackos, Helen Keller, and many others clearly demonstrate that the best performance is within you. Physical limitation can never become a stumbling block to success. Limitation is never in the body; it is always in the mind. There is a stellar performer within each of us, but most of the time we have handcuffed it with ego, fear, doubt, stress, and anxiety. None of us are born any luckier than anyone else. Career life gives a fair chance to everyone to excel, the difference is some bring out the stellar performer from within and some search to nurture it from externals. If you chase after success, it will elude you. You are chasing a shadow that will disappear in darkness. A job aspirant craving for a job does not get it. A young man wanting desperately to become a CEO fails in his endeavor. An entrepreneur obsessed with money never gets enough. All three fall short not because of incompetence, but because they are chasing something temporary that is outside.

The people who dared to dream and believe in possibilities have created this world. All inventions, discoveries, and achievements in human civilizations are results of believers and strivers who believed that success is within them, and there are no limits to their achievements. Never talk of success in future or past tense. "I will be successful when…" Always say I am successful. Success is within you, within me, and within everyone who is in their career life. The only difference is that for few the success within is awake and for majority of us we have allowed it to rest in peace.

There is a direct connection between your body and your mind. Physiology is a crucial component to success in every area of your career life. In the later chapters, you will read more about how to change your physiology for success. For now, repeat this mantra: I am successful and that is why I achieve. And now try to answer these questions again: What if you do not get success even after all the hard work? What if you toiled day and night, yet your competitor took your client? What if for 5 years you are doing everything to get to the director's position only to know your colleague got it? What if your business is thriving and you get to know your spouse company has relocated him to another city, where you would need to set up your business all over? Do you see a shift in your perspective?

This one mantra when used in career life will change your thinking and will create behaviors in you that will take you to massive results in the world around you. Every time you say to yourself I am successful that is why I achieve, you change your internal state of mind, which means you change your karmas for better results. When you feel successful from within your body language conveys a positive message to the outer world and to the universe.

When my husband transferred job to America, I had to quit my flourishing career. I was hugely successful in my work. Work was my first love. Now, if any of you have been a similar situation where you had to leave what you love the most, you know how it feels. Coming to

America on a dependent visa meant I could not continue to work for some years. I met many ladies from different countries, some who were doctors, engineers, and even MBAs like me. We all felt disheartened that they were not working while staying at home. Most of our talks revolved around boredom. I was frustrated too. I knew that no one except me could do anything about this situation. I had a choice: wait for success or activate the success within. I chose the latter.

During this time when I did not have a working visa, I enrolled in classes for enhancing my human resources knowledge. I studied, submitted articles to magazines globally, volunteered to facilitate free leadership training, and even started my first nonprofit dance and fitness class. I did everything that others in my situation were not doing. All this made me what I am today. It enriched me. As soon as I got my working visa, my career progressed upward. What I did wasn't anything extraordinary that someone else in my situation could not do. Anyone can achieve what he or she wants irrespective of the situation as long as you magnetize your mind with the thought that you achieve and that is why you are successful.

What would it feel like to know in your thoughts, heart, mind, and the very depth of your soul that you are born to be successful? To see that success is within you already? To know that no matter what happens with the corporate world, technology, economy, job status, business environment, or recruitment, you always have a secured future at all times? When you find that calling that speaks to you telling you that success of any kind is a journey, not a destination, you will look within. When looking for the answers to your personal questions, it's important to remember that everything you need to know is already inside of you. You just have to listen. There are many things we will gain and lose during our careers. If within us we are full of success, then we can always have these things again.

Don't waste your career life chasing something that is in abundance within you. Use that success within to manifest the results at your workplace. Activate the success within. Carry success with you wherever you go.

KARMA 7

Expedite Your Happiness

Procrastination comes in many forms. Some business people have trouble finishing their projects. They are always saying the following statements to themselves: "I will start a company when…"; "I will get the right job when…"; "I will start this project when…"; "I will change my ways when…" They don't complete their sentences. Most of the procrastination involves finding happiness. They say: "I will be happy when I get my new car, the promotion, another few clients, a new home, a new job, or start my business…" What are the sentences that you don't complete? What are the projects that you don't finish? What are the dreams that you have not realized?

In today's modern corporate world, if there's one thing that's missing, it is happiness. When I ask business leaders what they want, they first say they want to be successful. But when I dig further, they say they truly want to be happy. Success makes them happy. Happiness is the ultimate goal for every action we take. Whatever our definitions of happiness, we all want it and we search for it constantly. In fact, employees' happiness is an increasingly important aspect of the modern workplace. Companies are constantly revising their benefits toward cultivating a culture that offers remote work, healthcare, paid vacations, in-house fitness centers, healthy food, and much more. All these aim to keep employees happy. But are employees truly happy? Do you see your workplace thriving with happiness? It's worth taking a moment to consider from where happiness comes.

Why are some people happier than others? Is it that they've found what they love to do? Or, have they found a seemingly magical method for happiness? Sundar Pichai, the chief executive of Google Inc., said it best: "A person who is happy is not because everything is right in his life; he is happy because his attitude toward everything in his life is right."

There are many beliefs centered on workplace happiness. One belief is that happiness is bound to external success. It is bound with achievements and possessions. This belief can be quite fickle. Happiness is that which we cannot hold and cannot store. It has to be enjoyed and experienced in real time. Usually, when an event or situation is over, the happiness levels drop. If there is a salary increment or client deal signed today, we feel happy. But after 10 days, we find it difficult to achieve the same level of happiness. Happiness and unhappiness are part of the duality of existence. One follows the other, and they often move in cycles. If our happiness is because of external possessions—a new car, a job, or a new role—then we will be equally unhappy when these things are taken away from us. Many of us even postpone our happiness, waiting for that "aha" moment. Few know when that right moment will arrive. We search for this intangible state throughout our careers. We find it difficult to be happy at our workplace. We are looking outside of ourselves for the happiness that should be within us.

Let's turn to the story of the proprietor of a coffee shop who was busy on Saturday. His shop was very crowded, and the customers seemed unending. He had been on his toes since morning. Toward the evening, he felt a splitting headache surfacing. As the clock ticked away, his headache worsened. Unable to bear it, he stepped out of the shop, leaving his staff to look after the sales. He walked across the street to the pharmacy, to buy himself a painkiller to relieve his headache. As he strolled out of the shop, he casually asked at the checkout, "Where is the head pharmacist? He's not at the counter today!" The girl replied, "Sir, he had a splitting headache and said he was going across to the coffee shop. He said a cup of hot coffee would relieve him of his headache." The man's mouth went dry and he mumbled, "Oh! I see."

This story brings home a great message: most of us look outside ourselves for something that we already have within us. How strange but true! The pharmacist relieves his headache by drinking coffee, and the coffee shop owner finds relief in a pain-relieving pill! People switch jobs in hope that a company will have a positive work environment, great opportunities, higher salary, and good benefits only to find themselves trapped back into finding happiness.

Very recently an associate of mine lost his job. When we met at a social gathering, I saw him looking tense and stressed. I heard he had been out of a job for a few months, and he also developed chronic respiratory disorders. Earlier he was in a job at a Fortune 500 company. He was doing well, earning a stupendous income. He invested his money to buy his dream home. Buying the home made him feel happy.

Things got slightly complicated later because of his high home mortgage and other expenses. At work, he wasn't feeling happy with his current position either. He accepted another job offer. Once again, he felt happy because of the higher salary and new job title. Within a year he got to know that the culture of the company wasn't conducive for his skills and ideas. He found another opportunity in a mid-size company that was growing fast. He took up a better role there, worked with them for a year and a half, and just before Thanksgiving the company shut down the department he was working for and he was laid off.

In his search for happiness, he landed up with stress and ill health. If he were truly happy within, he would have maintained a calm state of mind, and his karmas would have different. His search for happiness within his jobs and material wealth made him unhappy overall. Now I am not saying that one mustn't think of growth or look around for opportunities. Of course, we should. That's what career life is about—progress. What matters is *how* you are progressing. Are you progressing in a state of happiness or unhappiness? If you find yourself in the latter zone, then you are actually progressing not for growth, and you are only searching for happiness. You will only find it temporarily just like my colleague in the above story.

There is a reason I emphasize this. Let's consider you are progressing in a state of unhappiness. When in this state, you wake up lethargic, not excited about the day ahead. Thus, the mindset with which you start your day will determine your immediate next karma. Your karma will be limited, and you will not use your full potential at work. You are already exhausted. This slows down your growth, has an adverse effect on your health, and leaves you devastated. If an opportunity comes your way chances are you may miss it due to a disturbed state of mind. Your problems appear bigger than they are and you continue in this phase until you find happiness somewhere in some form.

But when you progress in a state of happiness, things are different. You wake up in the morning energized, and you look ahead to your day at work. A day that starts with high energy, focus, and determination will create feelings of serenity, joy, and passion. Your karma will be unlimited, and you will use your full potential at work. This speeds up your growth. Now when you get that job offer, new business client, increment, promotion, the feeling of happiness isn't temporary. It is because you were happy that you created your favorable situation. We take ourselves wherever we go. How you feel within is what creates your outer environment.

Any happiness that is dependent on someone or something else will always be temporary. In my interaction with corporate leaders and business owners, oftentimes I hear them say to me that they are happy or sad at work because of their boss or because of the number of clients they have. This is why when there is reorganization in the company, or the client list falls short, people get disturbed and anxiety levels rise. They hope that the next boss is good and keeps them happy. This thinking means we are giving the remote control of our happiness to another person. Your success, your goals, your desires, and your dreams all require you to be in a state of happiness. I have met numerous people who have it all in their career, but at the same time are miserably unhappy. Year ago, I worked with a boss in my field of leadership training. My boss was a well-known personality in her field at the time, but she was also extremely unhappy. She would often lose her temper, and she was impulsive, giving instructions on the spur of the moment. I realized you could be very smart and even get on the Guinness World Records, but be extremely unhappy at the same time.

Another controversial belief around workplace happiness is that being happy is about "positive thinking." Actually, it's more about cultivating a realistic attitude that accepts situations and people as they are. It's common for most of us to resist emotions like worry and sadness. But the truth of the matter is that you need sadness if you're going to have happiness. Just like you need darkness if you're going to have light. I know this from personal experience. I've seen people go through hardships and depression in business and corporate life, and yet turn their life around purely through their mindset. Don't worry if you think this doesn't sound like you. The good news is you can be one of those people. Those characteristics are largely learned. Being happy is possible, no matter how tough your days are.

One way to change your state from happiness to unhappiness is to do a self-audit. If you see your shoulders slumped, spine bent, face gloomy, and eyes looking down, then the enemies of success surround you. If you see your shoulders are rounded back, spine tall, face radiant, calm mind, and eyes looking forward, then the friends of success surround you.

Right now, as you read this book, stand up nice and tall, smile, look straight ahead, and say to yourself with energy, "I can and I will!" Now say it one more time with boundless enthusiasm: "I can and I will!" Do you see the difference in how you feel? Do you feel more energetic, more alive, and stronger? Even a slight change in motion alters emotions. Let's not wait for someone or something to happen to change our emotions and motion. You have the power to do it right away. Repeat this mantra as many times in a day and see the results.

Your internal happiness is brought forth to people around you by your posture, eye movements, walk, and breathing. Internal happiness brings a huge shift in your emotion. Change in emotion is followed by the change in energy level, physiology, karma, and results. If you want to achieve massive results, then happiness has to be unlimited within yourself. It has to be a lasting happiness. If you are waiting for happiness to come to you because of some person or event, you are actually making success wait. It will take you longer to achieve your goals. We all have only a limited time period in our careers. Would you not want to speed up growth as well as maintain serenity? If you desire to be independent, then do not be dependent on outer environments for your happiness.

In today's business world, the wait for happiness is endless. People are waiting for bonuses, growth, clients, homes, cars, promotions, and many other things to make them happy. Soon one day they wake up to realize they are at the end of their careers. The phase of life where you should be happy passes away sprinkling on you only few showers of happiness. I have met extremely few people in who are happy at work all the time in the corporate and business world. But I feel blessed to have coached people to cultivate internal happiness.

My husband finds it ironic that I could be so happy at work and feel energetic. In fact, many times I have heard him say to me that very few find happiness at work like I do. When I look at today's work culture, I agree with him. When everyone is focusing outwardly for happiness, it is bound to be short-lived. How do I know this? Well, test it for yourself. If today you get that big promotion, that big client deal, or salary increase, you feel you are happy, right? Internally you are feeling full of joy. Within a few minutes you get a call from home that a family member is hospitalized and is in serious condition because of an accident. Now what is the internal state—happy or sad? You waited for six months, maybe a year to achieve your goals and experience happiness. Why didn't the happy feeling stay longer?

Happiness is a natural state and it is within us 24 h, 7 days of the week. Even in the midst of all work pressures, one can and should maintain their natural state of happiness. It has nothing to do with the external circumstances. It is an internal feeling, an intense joy that arises for nothing, just because of the fact that we are. For many people, happiness becomes conditional. They say, "I will be happy only if such a thing happens, or when I become something, or when I acquire something." But getting or not getting depends on our efforts along with luck, destiny, talent, circumstances, karma, etc.

Most of us who think that happiness is conditional spend most of our lives at work in an unhappy state. Only when we remove the conditions and decide to be happy, does happiness come to us. I follow a simple mantra in my work life. Rather than thinking when I achieve I will be happy, I tell myself, "I will be happy while I achieve." Most people postpone their happiness waiting for something to achieve. I expedite my happiness while I achieve because my happiness brings me success, my happiness comes from within, and my happiness is ongoing, permeating through all of the parts of my life.

People are only as happy as they believe they can be. You can choose to be happy. Every single day you wake up with choices. There are at least two ways of being happy each day: change your inner environment or your change your outer environment immediately. Can you make sure that the economy is doing well, that there are no layoffs, that there are plenty of resources, that office politics are minimal, that your clients give you business, that there are growth opportunities, or that your increments are permanent? You may not be able to change these external circumstances, but you can change your inner environment so that whatever arises from the outside does not derail your happiness.

Some time ago I led a workshop at a Fortune 500 company in San Jose, California. As I walked into the building, I suddenly recollected the number of attempts I had made to secure a job at this company. Back then my life had been focused on controlling the outer environment to keep up with my job and salary, compete for promotion, and dodge layoffs. There was a constant feeling of unhappiness within. Fast forward, I feel blessed now to create an impact on many leaders globally. How did I achieve this? What did it take to move ahead with persistence?

I found a way to be happy while achieving. In the midst of all my problems, I fine-tuned my inner environment to move ahead with speed and serenity. I would repeat this mantra to myself: "Be happy while achieve." Then every cell and nerve in my body compelled itself to move, and I believed that I am not dependent on outside resources for success.

That day, as I entered the building to conduct Leadership Through Mind session, I realized how much fulfillment I felt. As I continued into the building, observing the pleasant décor, I was amazed at the greeting of the receptionist. She immediately smiled and mentioned how Leadership Through Mind techniques helped her complete her overdue marketing and administration course. Being a single mom, she had delayed her coursework under the pretext of not having enough time while taking care of her daughter. All this led her unhappiness within herself. Soon she practiced the art of being happy while achieving. Today, her face looked proud—you should have been there to witness it. As I settled into the conference room, participants began to enter the room. One gentleman who was a manager shared his success story with me. Just a year before he was struggling to move up in the organization. Every day when he would come to work, he was unhappy with his progress. After he learned to harness LTM mindset techniques, he became more successful. I felt honored to see the progress of all of the people within my workshop.

Speaking of progress, when you were asked where do you see yourself in the next few years, what was your response? Are you there now? How long did it take you to get there? I can almost assure you that each of you will move ahead in your career. The most important question is how? The journey to your goal is more important than the goal itself. How did you reach your goals, with happiness or unhappiness? Overall in your career, have you been happy most of the days at work or unhappy? I would like you to take a moment to answer these crucial questions and reflect upon them before reading ahead. Often times in an attempt to be happy we are looking at changing others, altering situations, changing our careers, or moving cities. We look for happiness outside and that is why we blame people, situations, economy, government, boss, management, client, weather, and even God.

Expedite your happiness each day. Happiness and unhappiness are states of mind. Whatever is your state of mind is what you bring with you at your workplace. No company sets its foundation on negativity and unhappiness. Negativity and unhappiness enters into business because of each of us. The emotions you bring to work every single day build up over time and create your work environment. Happiness and sadness are emotions you create. No one is responsible outwardly for your state of emotions. You decide every morning what you want to create. This is probably quite scary for many, because it means that there are no longer any excuses that could justify cultivating unhappiness.

Happiness is free. It's available on demand. Don't bind it with career materialism. Let your happiness be unlimited at all times. The best way I generate happiness on demand is be humble, loving, tranquil, calm, and proud while avoiding professional grudges. Being in a state of happiness does not make you inactive. It keeps you healthy, both mentally and physically. In context of our fast-paced lives, your happiness is critical to creativity, innovation, confidence, and success in every arena. If you're happy without depending on outer environment, you attract success. People like to deal with people who possess an overall happy personality, which means you attract more clients, your team relates with you more, and you increase your profits. A person who is happy has a higher chance of achieving success. Every aspect of your career and business improves, including productivity, performance, sales, promotion, and profits.

I believe if you perform your dharma with complete honesty and give it your best, then you experience internal happiness. Keep your eye on your duty and don't worry about what you will or will not get in return. Performing your dharma is the main reason you are in the career life. It gives you eternal peace of mind that you have given all you had to fulfill your dharma. We must perform our own dharma, and not neglect it. Fix your mind on your dharma without getting distracted by outer events. Dharma performed conscientiously will bring unlimited happiness in your life.

Don't tie your happiness to external events. Choose to be happy in every situation and every moment of your career life. You are responsible for your happiness. Never give anyone else the responsibility to control your happiness. We often believe that we need to be successful and wealthy be happy. Instead, empower yourself with the inner belief that you can choose to be happy no matter what the circumstances. This is the secret to lasting happiness in your career.

KARMA 8

Meditate for Success

With the hectic pace and demands of modern work life, many people feel stressed and overworked. It often feels like there isn't enough time in the day to get everything done. Our stress and tiredness make us unhappy, impatient, and frustrated. It even affects our health. Soon our dreams and goals get buried under the tension. Soon your career ends, and you have not achieved your goals. In the limited time you have in this phase of your life, you want to achieve success with speed and serenity. Keep this mantra in mind—I will return to it later in this chapter: Success is always achieved forward, but worked backward. To take control of your future, you must learn to meditate your way to success.

Around 15 years ago, I was appointed Regional Human Resource Manager at a well-known international chain of restaurants in India. When I took over the role, the company was not experiencing growth due to strong labor unions created voluntarily by the employees. If you have ever worked in a unionized workplace, you would know that a union agency acts as an intermediary between its members and the business, and there is limited scope of communication between management and employees. In a few months, I gauged the pulse of the problem. However, I wasn't able to break through the barrier of unions. At every stage there seemed a new obstacle.

To establish my credibility, and make the company hit skyrocket success, I made eradicating the union imperative. But whatever I did never seemed enough. Months passed and I felt we barely made any progress in this area. One day while sitting in a coffee shop, thinking about this issue and feeling disheartened, I stumbled upon an article from the *Washington Post* on how seeing in the mind is believing it can happen. It said that before a single event has begun, a single point awarded, a single shot contested, the Olympic competitors have already lived the games. They've felt their hand raised, swelled with pride as the national anthem played, felt the medal hang and tug at their neck.

"Every night I visualize myself winning the Olympics," said Kayla Harrison in the *Post* article. This caught my interest, and I did some further research about other successful people's meditative approaches. Consider a few of these examples that appeared in *Entrepreneur Magazine*:

- Boxing legend Muhammad Ali was always stressed the importance of seeing himself victorious long before the actual fight.
- As a struggling young actor, Jim Carrey used to picture himself being the greatest actor in the world.
- Michael Jordan always took the last shot in his mind before he ever took one in real life.

What I understood from this was that all top performers, regardless of the profession, know the importance of picturing themselves succeeding in their minds before they actually do so in reality. How about you? Every single day, do you take the time to visualize your success and achievement? Do you picture yourself having the perfect client meeting, of success in the project, of achieving that big goal, of getting triumph during a difficult phase in business, of making it big, of moving ahead to that next position, or the best team? I tried hard, but I just could not visualize as the top performers did. The pictures would come and vanish shortly after.

Though I wanted to see myself in an environment where we were union free—that I have achieved accolades for my performance, that we are a great team, that our company is flourishing, that I am progressing—the pictures wouldn't stay long. This made me further disheartened. From all my research and readings on visualizing success, I was definitely convinced that there is some scientific reasoning behind how our brain functions and why meditative visualizing is effective. So I wanted to learn this art and try it before giving up on it. Paulo Coelho de Souza, the Brazilian novelist said, "When you want something, all the universe conspires in helping you to achieve it." Well, that was exactly what happened. I wanted to eliminate unions, and I wanted to learn the art of visualizing this.

One Saturday morning, one of my aunts came to visit us at home. This aunt was a certified yoga and meditation instructor. I was not interested in yoga and meditation and thought it to be a waste of time just like many of us. She came to invite us for the inauguration of her new yoga center. My mom insisted I come with her. That day they were offering complimentary 10-min meditations. As the instructor was guiding us through a meditation process, my mind drifted to the union problem. As the instructions got clearer, so did my problem. In those 10 min, I got some clarity about a couple of pressing union problems. I did not pay further attention to the meditation part, but I decided to use whatever little clarity I received to address the issue at my work.

One action led to another and what followed was a series of courtroom hearings, meetings with management and the union, all of which ultimately lead to a successful removal of the union. This led to my promotion, which included a raise and a new job title. As much as I resented it, I did admit that something worked that day during the meditation. I did not know what. Thereafter I tried this process in few other aspects of my job and yes, it helped me almost all the time. Slowly I derived my own way to perform meditation in ways that don't take up much of my time as well as give me the result. As my career unfolded, I had mixed feelings about it. I had heard that professional life was all about jobs, teams, peers, management, business, paycheck, and building skills. I also knew this from traditional leadership books that emphasized goal setting, time management, and knowledge that careers are about achievements, success, ambitions, and growth. What I did not realize was that our careers are first about our inner perspective.

Many people in business or corporate life complain that it is very difficult to concentrate our attention and focus fully on the work. There is so much pressure from everywhere to perform and deliver results. Then there are fears that artificial intelligence (AI) will take our jobs. We seem to be pulled in all directions. Technological innovation is not the main reason that employees are not productive at their highest level. Employees aren't productive because we have forgotten to take care of our inner lives. We are innovating outside, but stagnating within. We aren't connected with ourselves. We aren't able to take control of our future, but we are supposed to design the company's future. The being is more important than the doing. If the being is distracted, and stressed, the doing will be below the desired level. Your karma—your action—is because of your mindset.

Leaders of the future need to have values, vision, and purpose. Add awareness, responsibility, and self-belief, and we have a powerful leader. When you learn to manage the "self," you manage the future. It is you that will step into the future. Let's try this simple exercise to examine the "you" of the future. Read the exercise, and then with your eyes closed, practice it.

Ok, so here it is. Sit back and relax. Close your eyes and take five deep breaths. As you return to breathing normally, step into the future. It's 5 years from now. You are still carrying the baggage of your limited beliefs, worries, and stresses. How do you look? What's your body posture like? Have you achieved what you wanted to achieve in 5 years? From here, go 10 years ahead. You are still carrying the same baggage, and added to this, you have self-doubt, distraction, and fear. How do you look? See your future self vividly in your mind. Where are you going? Is it toward success, thriving, and flourishing? Or is it toward massive debt, a heart attack, serious illness, and severe restrictions in your future? Do you want go to this place where it is very likely that you will wind up if you don't make a change?

Now see your future self where you are traveling without the baggage of self-doubt, worry, and anxiety. What positive and awesome things has your positive attitude brought you in 5 years and in 10 years? See it all in your mind. Take a few breaths, open your eyes, and repeat these words aloud: Future by choice not future by chance. A future by choice is possible. You have to only manage your inner self, and your future will be managed.

Many top business leaders meditate, and they attribute a huge part of their professional success to it. Today companies like Google, Target, and many others invest in meditative practice. Just spending 10 min listening to what the universe wants to unfold for you can go a long way to help you handle your day. When you have a pressing problem, need guidance in decision-making, want an idea for your business, need confidence for a presentation, or want to resolve conflict, meditate on it. You will be amazed at the results. This is because it slows down your mind, creating calm space within. Only in silence can you hear what your inner self is telling you. It's the best guide ever. Whether you own a small business or work for a corporate giant, it's the ideal time to introduce a meditative practice to help you toward success.

Some feel that meditation takes up too much of their time. But in reality, meditation gives us more time by making our minds calmer and more focused. It is a simple process for busy professionals. It brings you back to the importance of being instead of doing. I simply consider meditation as a process to "think deeply." As corporate leaders and business owners, we are tuned to think deeply about everything that impacts our careers. So this deep meditative thinking helps us create unstoppable success.

Moreover, I once thought that meditation was the exclusive province of gurus and pundits. I soon realized that it's simply a practice that activates our inner self to create awareness. Nor does meditation demand sitting with your eyes closed in exact positions. To think about your friends and family, do you have to close your eyes and sit in a particular posture? Likewise, to connect with your inner self and be aware, you don't necessarily have to close your eyes. It's not just about visualizing, it's about feeling and experiencing. It means you are connecting with yourself and the universe at large. In the world of business, you are spending so much of your time connecting with hundreds of people that don't you take just 10 min to connect with yourself. Has work made us so busy that it has disconnected us from ourselves? As Deepak Chopra put it, "Meditation is all about connecting with your soul. Part of maintaining your well-being is taking the time to disconnect from the outside to go within."

Let's turn now to two processes that I use with business leaders to help them understand the benefits of meditation. I call the first process DREAM. Each letter in the acronym represents a karma (or action) that we may take to achieve success through meditation. This process can be done anywhere and anytime—at your desk at work during the day or at home at night before you fall asleep. Here are the DREAM steps:

- Detach yourself for a few minutes from all your issues and problems, and be in silence. Only in silence will you be able to hear the sound of the unspoken.
- Relax by concentrating on your breath. Let thoughts flow naturally. Every time your thoughts wander, refocus on your breathing.
- Express your inner ideas and feelings by talking to yourself. Ask and answer questions like these: "What is it that I want? For what am I grateful?"
- Attend to your choices. Check the quality of your thoughts. What type of thoughts are you having? Pay attention and be choosy to select the healthiest thoughts to carry with you.
- Merge yourself into the universe and repeat this mantra: "I am a powerful being." Repeat this mantra as many times in a day you can. It will create a positive mental vibration.

I call the second process that I use with business leaders the TRAIL method. TRAIL stands for Think Reverse and Influence Leadership.

This method has proven to give a great deal of clarity to my clients. Success is always achieved forward, but worked in reverse. With TRAIL you need to work backward from your end goal. It is a two-step process:

- **Step 1.** Outcome: When you have a goal for a project, first decide the end outcome. For example, let's say you want your business to grow. Rather than moving ahead with your strategies, write down what you see your business at the peak of its growth. Then we must work backward to achieve each of the elements that epitomize your business' peak of growth.
- **Step 2.** Chunk it down. Take a step-by-step approach. Ask and answer questions like this: "What are the elements— step-by-step—that need to happen to achieve the end outcome?" Then, when you accomplish the first step, move on to the next. Visualize what the project will look like just before the end goal is accomplished and right after it is accomplished.
- This is how I incorporated DREAM and TRAIL to help my company become union free:
- I made my one revolutionary resolution for the next 3 months: to get the company to be union free.
- In the DREAM stage, I took a few minutes each day to meditate on how it would feel for us to be union free, to have positive employee relations, and company growth. I imagined myself there and how it would feel.
- I now started working things out in reverse way. On a huge chart, I chunked the matter down, separating it into the BIG goal and subgoals.
- I worked these subgoals backward: I examined what our company would look like just before the company gets union free and what it would look like afterward. Answer: we need to win the court case in our favor. What is to happen just before we win the court case in our favor. Answer: we needed more than 58% of the workers to vote against the union. But I could not accomplish this step if I did not meet the challenge of the first

step, which is to build more trust between the employees, the management, and myself.

• Once this map was clear, I worked forward from the first step to the last step to reach to the BIG Goal.

The DREAM and TRAIL processes gave me courage and clarity to move ahead and break through my very first big workplace obstacle The DREAM meditation helped me gain a positive shift in my emotions and energy. The method helped me think through and plan out my path toward my goals.

Figure 8.1 illustrates the processes that I emphasize here.

Today most of us are engrossed in working toward results that we do not take time to meditate on how we reach the outcome. How will you reach success and achieve? In today's busy work life, you cannot depend on anyone other than yourself for motivation. You have to derive your own techniques to keep moving ahead toward achievement. When practiced daily, my clients and I benefit from the DREAM and TRAIL methods in the following ways:

1. They create positive inner vibrations that calm, activate, and energize our actions.
2. They give us power to control our minds.
3. They set the pace for the day.
4. They slow down our thoughts.
5. They help us maintain a calm state of mind needed for decision-making.
6. They prime us for success.
7. They enhance our focus, which doubles our productivity.

Figure 8.1 *A simplified model of the DREAM and TRAIL processes.*

8. They bring about greater emotional stability.
9. They are great stress-busters.
10. And, most importantly, they empower us to think about ourselves, to ourselves, and for ourselves. This is something we have forgotten while pursuing our goals and dreams.

When you meditate on a goal and imagine it accomplished, the energy that you create and bring it with you to your present acts as a driving force. Even as little as 10 min of meditation a day de-clutters the mind and restores focus and clarity. The people I know who meditate are one step ahead of others. It's time to get in contact with the real person who exists behind the roles we play. Success can be achieved with speed and serenity. It's just a matter of a few minutes each day.

KARMA 9

Unlock Your Inner Power

Have you ever failed? Can you think of the reasons why you failed? I am sure we all have our reasons: time management, the economy, skills, knowledge, confidence, and the list goes on. Failure often all comes down to one word: resources. Many of us fail in the projects within our careers because we lacked resources. Each of us has so much inner resources for our success. This inner resource is called *shakti*. We are all born with shakti. Shakti simply means inner power or strength, and we are all blessed with it in plenty. Those who tap their powerful inner resources will move ahead without depending on outer resources.

Does that mean people who seem to have more resources than others will succeed most of the time? No, it does not. If you have any doubts about this, let me introduce you to one of my clients named Marsha. Marsha was born with a silver spoon in her mouth. She had a loving family, received the best education, and had the least struggles in life. She wanted to get into business. She had resources, time, support, money, and a good professional network. Yet, after 3 years of being in business, Marsha was on the verge of ceasing to operate her company. This is when Marsha met me.

Marsha explained her story to me, and we did five sessions of coaching. Today Marsha is not only back in business but also expanded her venture in international markets too. I am sure like Marsha you too know people who have the best of the best, but don't achieve much. Yet, there are people who barely have any resources, but reach the pinnacle of success. We read about people who made it from rags to riches. What about people with disabilities who established themselves? How do some people make it and some don't? What is the difference between people who have the best of resources but aren't getting anywhere, and people who barely have resources but are making it there? The difference is because some are looking for resources outside, and some are looking for resources within themselves.

All of the resources that are necessary for progress are within you. You are born resourceful. We all originate from the universe. The universe is powerful and resourceful, and the same has been bestowed upon us. Each of us has so many inner resources to move ahead successfully. Outside resources are limited, but inner resources are limitless. Outside resources can decrease, but inner resources always increase. Inner resources generate outer resources. We must tap into our *shakti*, or inner power, to move ahead without depending on the outer resources.

Think of one career goal you have wanted to achieve, but couldn't. Now think of the reasons you could not achieve it? Most of the time you know what you want and why you want it. Yet, you get stuck because of a lack of inner resources.

You want to do it, and you feel motivated, but every time your mind keeps asking you "How?" you shut down. You keep asking yourself questions like this: How can you do it without a certificate course? How are you going to do it without money, without people, or without time?" Days become weeks, weeks become months, and soon years have passed by and you aren't where you want to be.

Our inner power is like fire. Released for constructive purposes, you inner power spreads like a blaze. This can be seen through the lens of quantum physics. The atoms that make up your body are constantly vibrating at a very fast rate. If you are in a positive state of mind, you will be vibrating at a very high frequency, and this makes it very difficult for any negative energy to infiltrate you. But if you are unhappy or depressed and vibrating at a very low and slow frequency, then you are open to all types of negative energy that will only serve to bring you even further down.

So that is why it is important to harness positive inner power within you to become resourceful. A resourceful person can achieve regardless of the situation. Remember each of us is self-made: we are either self-made successful people or self-made failures. But we are self-made.

Recognize and use your positive shakti. Don't slow down, and don't get off the proverbial highway just because of rejection and dejection. Rejection and dejection are a part of career and business life. You have this time with you to do whatever you dreamt of. Your inner power is the magnet with which you can attract what you want. Step into your greatness, step into your true self, and all resources will draw toward you.

A few years back, I was delivering a talk at a leadership seminar organized at my daughter's high school. In that seminar, I had the privilege to meet with veterans and active duty men and women. We had an interesting conversation around resources where I got to know that in a soldier's life the resources are never perfect. They do not know the time the enemy will attack, or what equipment the enemy has, or how much manpower they have. But regardless of everything, they still have to win the battle. The reason they said they are able to do yet go ahead is because they are proud of their country and believe in their inner resources.

Within our careers we are always concerned about resources: human capital, natural resources, financial resources, and marketing resources. Everything seems tight and limited. We feel as if we are tied to these outer resources, and we can't move ahead because of short supplies. I often wonder, are we really dependent on these outer resources for our success? Is it possible to move ahead without sufficient resources? Can anyone achieve success with tight resources? Let's look at how three inspirational people marshaled their inner power despite having limited outer resources.

1. Dashrath Manji (also known as the Mountain Man) was a man who lived in the village of Gehlaur in the state of Bihar in India. He was famous for using just a hammer to cut down mountains. He was a poor laborer who single handedly carved a path through a mountain using only a hammer and chisel. While his resources were limited, his achievement was great.

2. Bethany Hamilton, the famous surfer, returned to the sport after losing an arm in a shark attack. Hamilton was a top young amateur when a 14-foot tiger shark in Kauai, Hawaii, attacked her at the age of 13 in 2003. But she was back surfing within a month. Few expected Hamilton to reach the top level of the sport while surfing with just one arm. While her resources were limited, her achievement was great.

3. Dhirubhai Ambani was born in a poor family in India. But he rose from humble beginnings to create India's largest industrial empire, and in the process, became one of the world's richest men. He too did not let meager resources stop his achievement.

How tight were resources for these people? Was success even imaginable? Were the outer resources sufficient for them? Anyone can be resourceful, but only if they decide to use their inner power.

Do you sometimes feel like your energy is dried up or depleted, like you just want to quit? Or, do you feel exhausted trying to overcome obstacles at work? Or, maybe you are tired of the routine of your career? Then it's time to activate the shakti within you.

Within each of us, there are both positive shakti and negative shakti. Both are needed to balance our career life. For example, a healthy amount of doubt can help you gain a clearer perspective on things. It is when we allow the negative shakti to overpower us that we fall short on ourselves, on our results, and on our achievements. The negative shakti pulls us down and does not allow us to be resourceful. To generate resources you must activate the positive shaktis. With these positive shaktis you will be able to generate the resources that will take you closer to your goals. Table 9.1 illustrates the varieties of both positive and negative shaktis.

When positive shaktis are activated internally, they create tremendous inner resources that lead you to generate outer resources. Here's an example. You have a keen desire to grow your business or climb up the corporate ladder. When you look around you, reality speaks a different language. You see a lack of budget, lack of manpower, tremendous

Table 9.1 *Positive and Negative Shaktis*

Positive Shakti	Negative Shakti
Belief	Doubt
Confidence	Uncertainty
Peace	Worry
Love	Hatred
Happiness	Unhappiness
Greatness	Incompetence
Action	Inaction
Gratitude	Thanklessness
Hope	Anxiety
Courage	Fear
Interest	Indifference
Patience	Frustration
Charity	Greed

competition, changes in government policies, and other factors. You have all the necessary skill sets, but yet aren't able to move the needle much toward growth.

You have two options. Option one: wait for the resources to develop, lament over it, keep asking for help, and worry about your situation. Option two: awaken your positive shakti, your inner resources like confidence, interest, and happiness and with these inner resources, move everyday toward generating your outer resources. You will experience success when inner resources and outer resources come together. Outer resources may not in your control, but inner resources are.

When you awaken your inner shakti to become resourceful, you become a self-starter. You become enthusiastic and you pave your path. I was once invited to Dubai for an inspirational leadership talk. While on my way back to the hotel, I took a cab. This must have been one of the finest cabs I have ever traveled in so many years. The cab driver was friendly, and she offered me some water, soda, and chips at absolutely no cost.

By now I was impressed and curious. How does she manage to provide this "elite" service within her income? On conversing with her, I learnt that 5 years back she was barely making enough money by driving a cab. She was exasperated by competing for customers at the airport as there were tons of cabs lined up for the same. Every day she went home with barely any earnings. Then one day she read a line from an article that changed her life. It read, "you can either be a duck that complains or an eagle that flies high up in the sky."

From that day on she decided to be an eagle and design her destiny as a cab driver. She started to notice what other cabs lack, like cleanliness (both in and out), water, and extra services like sodas and chips. She built a service based on customer relations. She started small. First, she wrote a mission statement that read, "To help my customers reach their destination in the safest and most economical way." Then as customers increased and her earnings grew, she invested in these "elite" services. Soon she handed business cards to her customers who called her when they needed a ride. She no longer waits in line now. Things changed in her life the minute she turned to becoming resourceful.

Are you a duck or an eagle? What's the difference you may ask? Well, ducks quack and complain, but eagles soar above the crowd. You have to make this choice daily because resourcefulness requires conscious, purposeful choice. It means taking responsibility for self and for your career. It's a shift from a complaining mindset to an action mindset.

Some years back no one had heard of the Internet, cell phones, or driverless cars. Today our life is surrounded by these innovations. Somebody imagined these innovations and marshaled their inner power, expert knowledge, and technical skill to make it into a reality. Think about it. When you applied for a job, during the interview did you ask if the company had enough resources so that you could work efficiently? When you started your own business, did you tell yourself, "I will go ahead only if resources are in my favor." Probably not. The reason being, you had enough confidence in the initiative to which you were applying and in yourself.

If optimization is the key word today, then being resourceful is a highly valuable trait. Being resourceful is now a necessary mindset for today's generation of leaders and teams. It is not simply doing more with less. It is the realization with your inner self that you can do more with less. Resourcefulness has everything to do with your ability to get the most from yourself in every situation.

We have conned ourselves to believe that budget, teams, economy, corporate politics, salary, uncertainty, top management, peers, time, and everything we could possibly point our finger to is the root cause for our professional problems. But all of these factors are just an easy way of out of taking the blame ourselves. Resourcefulness has everything to do with your ability to get the most from yourself in every situation. Self-made people did not start out with money, privilege, or connections. It's far easier to throw out excuses and live a mediocre life.

Here's a story about a company that manufactured hair shampoo. The shampoo was packed in small plastic bottles and then packed in a large container to ship. The company was a start-up with very limited resources both in money and manpower. After a few weeks of selling the product, the company started receiving complaints that some of the shampoo bottles were empty. The company realized this was its fault and wanted to make sure that the mistake did not happen again. To ensure this, they would need more manpower to manually check each bottle before being packed in container. They were extremely tight and knew that hiring more hands was nearly impossible. After a lot of thinking on solutions, the owner came up with an idea. He brought two huge blowers and kept them near the assembly line. As soon as the plastic bottle passed the blower, any empty bottle would be blown off. This solved his problem until he was able to afford more manpower. Resourcefulness leads to resources.

Now let me tell you about Wilma Rudolph, an athlete who was born into poverty in the state of Tennessee. When she was 4 years old, she had double pneumonia with scarlet fever, which left her paralyzed with polio. She had to wear braces, and the doctor said that she would not be able to walk normally again. Her mother encouraged her and said that she could do anything she wanted if she only believed. Wilma said, "I want to be the fastest woman on this earth." In the 1960 Olympics, Wilma Rudolph, the former paralytic girl, became the fastest woman

Table 9.2 *List of Shaktis*

Dependable	Kind	Relaxed
Curiosity	Joy	Peace
Disciplined	Lively	Warm
Contentment	Grateful	Hopeful
Sympathy	Patient	Respectful
Energetic	Pleasant	Responsible
Calm	Precise	Powerful
Carefree	Happiness	Satisfied
Flexible	Hope	Action
Caring	Progressive	Charity
Cheerful	Sympathetic	Self-conscious
Clever	Tactful	Realistic
Giving	Sociable	Sensible
Confident	Thoughtful	Sensitive
Happy	Belief	Sentimental
Imaginative	Objective	Compassionate
Independent	Rational	Stable
Intelligent	Observant	Patience

on this earth by winning three gold medals in the 100-m race, 200-m race, and 400-m relay. Who would have believed that a paralytic girl could have won three gold medals in the Olympics? If Wilma can make it big, what more can we do with all that we have. We have tremendous resources within us. All we need to do is believe in ourselves that we are resourceful.

Success in your career depends on which shakti you choose daily. Choose wisely. Let me close with a list of shaktis (Table 9.2). Take a moment and note which ones you wish that you had more. Think about one a week. Then, like an eagle, use your inner power to obtain these shaktis so you can soar.

Who doesn't have work life struggles? Who has perfect resources? Resources never seem sufficient. But there is never a shortage of inner resources. Get your desired outcome by increasing your inner power. Each of us enters our careers with a wealth of inner resources. But we rarely use a fraction of this wealth. We look around for solutions, we blame company and leadership, we talk to people about problems, we feel depressed about the situation, but not once do we put in the effort to create the resources by tapping inner resources.

When you awaken to your full shakti, you become an unstoppable force. You are more radiant. Resources fluctuate. Resourcefulness persists because it's within you. The only question is this: Are you ready to dive into your success? Your answer should always be, "Yes!"

KARMA 10

Become a Possibility Finder

There are two types of people in the workforce: Problem solvers and possibility finders. Both are needed. But possibility finders have an edge. They not only solve a problem, but they also look beyond and find possibilities. No matter what is happening in your career, be in the present moment. Accept that whatever is happening is for your best. Only then will you be able to make the best in any situation and find possibilities.

When you think of a possibility finder, what comes to your mind? To me a possibility finder is like the younger son in the following very short parable. One day a father gives a gift to each of his sons. To the older son, he gifted a bicycle, and to the younger son, he gifted a basket of horse dung.

"Only a bicycle! But I wanted a motorbike!" said the older son.

"If my father has given me a basket of horse dung, then surely there must be a horse to follow," said the younger son.

The older son always saw the downside of things, and the younger son always saw the upside of things. Possibility finders can see fortune despite what may seem like misfortune. They can make sense of the nonsense happening in the world. The agony today is that most of us have become so busy finding and solving problems that potential as possibility finders has become buried under our weight of mental stress. When we only focus on the problem and its solution our focus becomes narrow and limited. Success demands a wide vision.

The setting sun creates darkness on all sides. But just as the sun sets, another light begins to ascend. This light is that of the full moon. This is a sign of nature. When one possibility ends, another begins. The business world is full of wonderful possibilities. From every failure emerges the chance of new success. In fact, more than half of the Fortune 500 companies and many entrepreneurs thrived even during a recession. It takes an eye to find and take advantage of these opportunities. To have this kind of an eye to find possibilities, you need to cultivate an FBI mindset:

1. Find the best in everything.
2. Back up why with how.
3. Influence everything and everyone.

Having an FBI mindset and being a possibility finder requires accepting the ubiquity of your situation. Accept that whatever happened, it happened for the best, and then search for greater possibilities. The moment you accept the situation, your state of mind becomes relaxed.

As I write about the FBI state of mind, I am reminded of another short parable I read during my elementary years at school about a Chinese farmer. Once there was a poor Chinese farmer who worked his farm together with his son and their horse. When the horse ran off one day, neighbors came to say, "How unfortunate for you!" The farmer replied, "Maybe yes, maybe no." When the horse returned, followed by a herd of wild horses, the neighbors gathered around and exclaimed, "What good luck for you!" The farmer stayed calm and replied, "Maybe yes, maybe no." While trying to tame one of wild horses, the farmer's son fell, and broke his leg. He had to rest up and couldn't help with the farm chores. "How sad for you," the neighbors cried. "Maybe yes, maybe no," said the farmer.

Shortly thereafter, a neighboring army threatened the farmer's village. All the young men in the village were drafted to fight the invaders. But the farmer's son had been left out of the fighting because of his broken leg. People said to the farmer, "What a good thing your son couldn't fight!" "Maybe yes, maybe no," the farmer said.

This story helped me tremendously in my career. It taught me to work with an FBI mindset, where nothing seems as an advantage or a disadvantage. The whole process of events is an integrated one, and it's impossible to tell whether what happens is for the best or worst. Neither would we know the consequence of the misfortune or the consequences of good fortune. So we must find the best in everything. Instead of lamenting, we should see the incident as a stepping stone and concentrate on giving the right response to each situation. Back up why with how. When situations are favorable, do you ask yourself, why did such a good thing happen to me? When circumstances are against you, do you ask yourself, why did such a bad thing happen to me? When things are going well we generally do not why such a good thing happened to us.

But when things are not going our way or misfortunes hit us during our career life the first question we often ask is "Why did this happen to me?" We say, "If I did everything I could possibly do to make sure I am giving my best, then why is my name on the layoff list? If I have always done well for my people and company, then why am I not promoted? If I work tirelessly to get contracts, then why then do deals go to my competitors?" How often have you got a precise answer to your questions? I assume not many times. This practice of asking "why" drains out the most precious element needed for success, growth, decision making, and action: your Energy. When you are preoccupied with finding answers to why things happened in your career, you become drained of energy. This is accompanied by an unstoppable flow of negative thinking: an emotional flood that drowns you.

Now I am not saying that one must not question and analyze why things did not shape up the way they should. The simple point I state here is that things happen and we do not know why. Even if you analyze, obtaining the precise answer will be difficult. Most things happen because of past actions. Not everything comes packaged beautifully and that is why many opportunities remain unopened.

The success of Marvel Studios exemplifies the points that I make here. Marvel Entertainment had just recovered from bankruptcy when, in the year 1998, Sony Pictures approached them to buy theatrical screen rights for *Spider-Man*. Marvel Entertainment responded with a more audacious offer: Sony could have the movie rights to nearly every Marvel character for $25 million. Sony rejected the offer. Marvel Studios decided to self-produce its own movies with their characters, and Disney paid $4 billion dollars for the enterprise around the year 2010. A lost opportunity turned into a possibility. They went beyond the why. They harnessed the ability to influence the situation in a positive way. Each of us can influence the situation around us. Figure out the things you can change, and then change them. If you can't change something, learn to accept it quickly and then figure out the best way to move ahead.

From the moment you make a decision to step into a professional life, you're in the "career lifecycle." Think of the career life cycle as a cyclical, ongoing process. Here are the five stages of the career life cycle (illustrated in Figure 10.1 below):

- **Learning zone:** This is where you are fresh and hungry for knowledge. You develop skills. You are getting ready for your life's work.
- **Progress zone:** This is where we move ahead in your journey. Now you are a doer. You are taking on more responsibility.
- **Anxiety zone:** This is where you're definitely not a fresher, but you're also *far* from ready for graduation. You experience performance evaluations, peer competition, preparation, obstacles to growth, and doubts on self and others.
- **Growth zone:** This is where you begin moving ahead and generating a consistent source of income. You see rapid growth in both revenue and cash flow.
- **Stagnation:** Growth again comes to a halt. Here you decide of you want to move ahead or remain where you are until you exit.

These five stages are a continuous cycle within your career. When we encounter problems, if we aren't able to first accept them with an

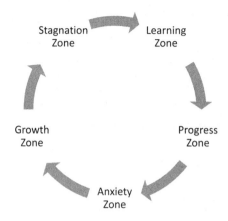

Figure 10.1   *The five stages of the career life cycle.*

F.B.I. mindset, then we get stuck in the anxiety zone rather than moving to the growth zone. Your past, present, and future are aligned to deliver the best for you today. If you look at the future changes or past events with a worried and motivated mindset, then will you take massive or mediocre actions? When you find yourself unsuccessful in the future, whom will you blame: technology, innovation, distributions, or yourself? To be ready for the uncertain future with both obstacles and growth, you must be willing to work on yourself and on your mindset in ways that will enhance your success. Acceptance is not a sign of weakness. It's a sign of strength, and a sign of growth. When you work for acceptance, you maintain a relaxed state of mind that enables you to make the best decision in a situation to move ahead in a different way that is beneficial for your growth.

Possibility finders first accept their circumstances, and then they look for and often find the best in virtually every situation. I know of many corporate leaders who have spent all their precious years complaining that there is no growth in their company. I know of business owners who tell me that cash flow is a problem because they are stuck. On the other hand, in the same company, there are people who have found growth opportunities. We are surrounded by possibilities. Our bodies respond and send out vibes when we accept or don't accept the situations.

Now I would like you to take a moment as you read this to establish a sense of acceptance. Think about a pressing problem at work. Think about why it happened. Talk to yourself about this problem. Talk about how it shouldn't have happened. Think how it may become better or worse. Now draw your attention to problems and solutions. Check in with your body. Ask and answer these questions:

- Are your shoulders are slouched?
- Is your spine bent?
- Has tension built up in your mind and body?
- Is your breath shallow?
- Has your heartbeat grown faster?
- Are your eyes are looking down?
- Do you have a sensation that you don't like dealing with whatever you are feeling?
- Do you wear a disheartening frown on your face?
- Do you feel enthusiastic?

Now, before switching to the next state, stand up and move around for at least 10 s. After moving around, you are now reading to experience a state of acceptance. Check in with your body again and ask and answer a different set of questions:

- Are your shoulders straight?
- Is your spine erect?
- Are your mind and body relaxed?
- Does your breath flow in an even pattern?
- Do your eyes look upward?
- Do you like to think about possibilities?
- Do you wear a smile on your face?
- Are you excited?

Both of these states have an impact on your mind and body. Likewise, these states are an outgrowth of your karmas (or actions). When confronted with problem at work, consciously make a shift in your thinking from nonacceptance to acceptance, and from problematizing to possibility finding. What we do is determined by our inner state.

It is up to you whether you choose to look only at the situation or look around it to catch possibilities it brings before they vanish. There are two ways out of any problem:

1. Accept what's happening, maintain a composed state of mind, and do something about it, or
2. Fight against it, keep asking why, be miserable, and disturb your state of mind.

We cannot control what comes to us from external factors, but we can control what goes on within us. Your rate of success is proportionate to the speed of your acceptance.

I have distilled all of this into what I called the ASAP method to become a possibility finder: analyze, shift, anchor, and practice. I share the components of the ASAP method with many of my clients, and now I will share them with you. As you become a possibility finder, ask and answer the following questions:

- **Analyze your current state:** What is your current state of feeling, emotions, and energy?
- Shift to the desired state: What is your current state of feeling, emotions, and energy?
- **Anchor your desired state:** When in that desired state, what unique anchor can you trigger to associate the anchor and the state together?
- **Practice the desired state:** How will you hold yourself accountable to practice your desired state?

Sometimes, we're so sure about how things are supposed to play out that we fight any detour from the plan. Something similar happened in the very initial years of my coaching and training practice. I was hired by a Fortune 500 company to deliver Leadership Through Mind sessions. We initially signed up for a pilot training. Based on the review, we would continue the session with other managers globally. After the 2-day pilot training, the reviews exceeded expectations.

I signed the contract for conducting this session for 100 managers globally starting first in Boston. My happiness knew no limits. It was a big contract. I accepted the contract and the happiness that came along. I completed the two sessions in Boston. I was enthusiastically preparing for the remaining sessions when I received a phone call from the Director of the department saying the session would need to be put on hold. There were some internal reorganizations taking place, and they now had to hold off on further trainings.

My heart sank. I did not know when the sessions would recommence and if they ever would. I did not accept the news and kept questioning why it was all occurring. I was working hard and diligently, and my sessions were appreciated. I spent 4 months worrying about this situation. But slowly I started to accept what had happened (it took additional 2 months for this acceptance to unfold). I moved ahead and reminded myself of the story about the young son who received a gift of a basket of dung from his father. If there is dung, then fortune will surely follow, I told myself.

I started planning, looking for more possibilities, and learning from the mistakes. I realized that every situation has a positive intention. In fact that is what it turned out to be. The training project of that company got shut down midway through, but it paved the way for me to facilitate the sessions for other teams with numbers that compared better to the earlier one. I gained a good understanding of how business should be planned and that helped me grow my consultancy.

Every situation is surrounded by possibilities. Stop judging the events as good or bad, positive or negative, and profit or loss. Rather, simply experience them and learn from them. Condition your mind to translate every event as feedback that empowers you to design your future. Expect the best and you will get it.

KARMA 11

Forgive

The business world is moving at jet speed. Look around your workspace, and you will observe that everyone is in a rush to get somewhere. Oftentimes, during this rush, we knowingly or unknowingly hurt a peer, upset someone, speak harshly, behave disrespectfully, or get into arguments. We usually do not pause to look back and mend broken relationships. These incidents haunt us even after retirement. We always remember that person who came in the way of our promotion or that competitor who took away our client, and we hold a grudge against them.

Right now if I asked you think of people with whom you have a professional grudge or resentment, I'm sure it wouldn't take even a few seconds for you to identify them within your mind. Every time you think of them, you become angry or sad. When you hold on to professional grudges and resentment there is a feeling of bondage, like an emotional chain. This chain binds you and prevents you from flying high because it makes you heavy from within, disturbing your state of mind. Holding resentments becomes your nature. You must learn to forgive, forget, and move forward.

Remember that to fly high like a kite, you must be light. Forgiving makes you light. It frees you from the emotional bondage. Forgiving is not easy. Unfortunately, we are prone to identify forgiving with only forgetting. Before reading ahead, can you tell yourself that today, right now, you will forgive someone that you have not been able to forgive in the past. Within your mind, forgive this person and send them best wishes.

I clearly remember an incident that took place between two professional women. Andrea was a Director and Joanna was a program manager reporting to Andrea. Often there was bitterness between them around day-to-day operations. Both failed to understand each other, and Andrea sensed Joanna was trying to take over her role. Finally, after many months, the Vice President had to intervene as it was affecting the cohesive functioning of the team. He explained and made an appeal to both professionals to rise above their differences and let bygones be bygones.

As they listened, Joanna saw the good sense of what he was saying. She softened, nodded in agreement, and turned toward Andrea with a smile and friendly glance. However, Andrea continued to be stiff and unbending. As he asked both of them their thoughts, Joanna spoke up ensuring these matters will not repeat. Andrea and Joanna smiled, agreed to let go of the issue, and they left the office. After a couple of months, Joanna resigned to join another organization. It turned out that Andrea had agreed to mend up, but internally she continued to hold grudges. The company lost a good team player and even today, after eight years when I met Andrea and Joanna, both remember the incidents matter as if it just happened yesterday. But, there is a huge difference. Andrea remembers it with bitterness and Joanna with sweetness as a learning experience because Joanna had forgiven, forgotten, and moved forward.

How many instances can you think of where you said it is okay, but did not really mean it? How many of us still hold on to those past professional grudges? When you think about them, do you remember them with bitterness or sweetness? If you remember the incidents with a feeling of bitterness, it means you haven't forgiven the person or yourself. Imprints of the person or the situation remain.

Holding on to professional grudges, resentment, and hurt is like holding a piece of hot burning coal in your hands and expecting others to get burnt. Feelings of resentment and grudges first destroy you before destroying others. We all get hurt in some way during our careers. It may be through peers, bosses, teams, or clients. Once we get hurt, we wait for our turn to reply back to that person either instantly or later. Unintentionally, we carry this burden of hurt, grudges, anger, and bitterness within our mind. Eventually, we end up carrying that person within our mind for so long, that our mind gets clouded with negative thoughts and anger for that person. It makes us sad and depressed. We talk about this person to whomever we meet. The incidents stay fresh as a wound, though we bandage it by saying, "Oh, I have forgiven him." But it's only a matter of time before the wound festers again. Once the bandage is removed, the bleeding starts again. We all have experienced this, haven't we? It does not end here. The wound gets infected and at times develops a foul odor. This odor is the energy you create. If you create foul energy, then this is what you carry with you everywhere. Holding to professional grudges are an obstacle we create on our path to success.

So why do we do this to ourselves? Most of the time it gives us comfort because we have someone to blame for the hurt and anger we feel. It's the boss, the colleague, or the government. And the story becomes stronger. Oftentimes we think we have let go and forgiven, but an event gives life to the whole experience again. The feelings, the anger, the resentment resurface, often clouding our judgment. If you really want to be stressed, all you have to do is hold on to the professional grudges. But if you want to move on toward bigger and brighter achievements, forgive. Forgiveness is not something you are doing for others, it is something we do for ourselves. It does not involve just verbally saying the word "Sorry."

In fact, most of the times, apologizing verbally to a person is not possible in a workplace because of the restrictions of our role, titles, and positions. Purely it's your actions that show if you have forgiven yourself, the person, and the situation. This is especially difficult when other people don't seek your forgiveness, or indeed when they are clearly in the wrong. I have noticed the toughest challenge people come across in their professional life is forgiving someone.

Once President Abraham Lincoln was asked why he showed compassion to the enemy when they should be killed. He answered that he destroys his enemies when he makes them his friends. Instead of settling scores, great leaders make gestures of reconciliation that heal wounds and get on with business. This is essential for reducing staff turnaround and creating a holistic work environment. Forgiveness requires flexibility, maturity, courage, and a positive attitude. It is not weakness. It is strength. Mahatma Gandhi said, "The weak can never forgive. Forgiveness is the attribute of the strong." When you let go and forgive you actually try to understand the weakness, fears, and insecurity of those on the other side of the issue. Mistakes and negative events occur constantly in our lives. At times, we bear the brunt of others' wrongdoing, and at times we wrong others.

Forgiveness does not mean putting up with unacceptable behaviors, and it is not a one-time act. It is not about running away from yourself and your true feelings. It's all about your inner strength and reflecting about the situation. It keeps your state of mind calm and helps you to take appropriate actions. One of the most courageous acts of leadership is to let go of the temptation to take revenge. How you respond to an event determines the next event in your life. What should you do when faced with betrayal, hurt, anger, or disappointment by peers, clients, or management? The most important aspect is to check on your ego. Ego is a silent killer of relationships. If we don't check our egos, then they become obnoxiously vast, and they block us from being able to empathize with others. When you put ego aside it means you value relationships more than being right or wrong.

Leadership is all about decision making, and forgiving is a decision that leaders must make. When leaders forgive, they let go of resentment, professional grudges, and ego, and build lasting relationships. Holding on to anxiety, grudges, and resentment undermines leadership and success. This has a direct effect on profits and results. How? The entire workplace is often drawn into the negativity of toxic relationships within which the employees have not forgiven each other and moved on from their pain. Forgiving means moving ahead, in your mind, and in your career.

We hear stories of great leaders who forgave their perpetrators. Nelson Mandela, Abraham Lincoln, and Gandhi are just few examples. People will wrong you at work, negative situations will arise, and people will hold resentment. What matters most is your state of mind. Make yourself such that no one can disturb your state of mind. Remember it's your mindset with which you will indulge in karmas that will bring forth your results. Always give prime importance to your outcome.

What is the outcome you want while in your professional life? Let me answer by telling you about the frog that participated in the race. One day all the frogs decided to show the people that they are mighty too. For this they challenged themselves to reach the top of a very high tower. A big crowd gathered around the tower to see the race and cheer on the contestants. The race began. No one in the crowd really believed that the tiny frogs would reach the top of the tower. They shouted, "Oh, way too difficult! They will NEVER make it to the top," and "Not a chance. The tower is too high." The tiny frogs began collapsing, one by one. But one continued higher and higher. This one wouldn't give up! And he reached the top. Everyone wanted to know how this one frog managed such a great feat. His secret? This little frog was deaf! Not being able to hear the doubters and the encouragers made this little frog single-minded in his focus on his goal.

Similarly, while in business, people will tell you words that will hurt you, and there will be situations where you will feel wronged. Be like this little frog whose only focus is on his goal: to reach the top. Those who let professional grudges affect them will slip down like the other frogs in the story. Because when you concentrate on people's actions and words, you are distracting yourself from your goal. You destroy yourself from within. You make yourself heavy when you should be like a light kite flying high.

I have helped many organizations start what I call a "Reflection Tree." This helped leaders and their teams put their egos aside and reflect on their karmas and thoughts to build great bonds with their team. This is how it works. We designate a space in the office. This space should be simply designed—it does not need cost a lot to set up this space. Within this space, there is an artificial tree or images of trees. When anyone is angry, upset, or low because of another's wrongdoing, or they wrong others, they can find solitude in that space amidst the Reflection Tree, or, they can treat the space as neutral territory and discuss their situation with their coworkers. During this time, they can follow a three-step forgiveness:

- **Forgive self:** Often we forgive others but not ourselves. Forgiving yourself helps you let go.
- **Forgive others:** Cultivate the attitude of letting go to break the cycle of negativity.
- **Forgive situation:** Believe that whatever happened was for the best and move on.

Go to the Reflection Tree until the matter is resolved within you. The results are long lasting. My clients tell me that whenever there are work conflicts, their people go to the Reflection Tree to reflect and discuss without much management intervention, and, most of the time, the conflict is successfully resolved. This idea of the Reflection Tree has helped to reduce staff turnover and create a holistic work environment. Unless it's a legal issue, things are calmly handled. Resolving conflicts and bitterness at work is the first step toward taking ownership, a quality we all look for in others.

Forgiveness practice is about liberating your own feelings and finding meaning in the worst of events. So you are truly practicing forgiveness for yourself. Refusing to forgive is one of the roots of escalating conflict, which causes a downward spiral. The biggest barrier to growth and progress is holding on to resentment.

Now, if you are thinking that I am a person who must have easily forgiven everyone who has wronged me or hurt me, well I wish that were the case. But I want to make it easier for others and myself to embrace forgiveness. Here's a formula that may help us. It's called FORGET.

- **FOCUS on change:** As soon as you feel resentment, change your focus on something, which is more productive to your team and work.
- **OWN:** Take ownership of your situation, let go of resentment, and create goodwill.
- **REFLECT:** Every night empty your mind of the little hurts and grudges you have accumulated during the day, and reflect on positive outcomes while working to move on.
- **GET CLEAR:** Clear your mind of the memories of anger, resentment, hurt, and bitterness.
- **ENRICH YOURSELF:** Whenever you feel resentment toward a colleague or situation, put a cent into your piggy bank and pledge forgiveness, and you may be amazed at your accumulated riches.
- **THINK:** Order your mind to forget the unnecessary thoughts and memories, which can only cause pain and distance you from the people.

You can convert every experience at work into an enriching process, or you can use it to become more resistant toward life. You must choose. I urge you as leaders to think of someone who has wronged you or hurt you. What does it mean for you to forgive them? What would you have to do to forgive?

Remember, years later, you won't be remembered at your workplace for the kind of car you drove, positions held, or the salary taken. But you will be remembered for asking how many bridges of relationship you built and how many hearts you healed. Forgiveness is a very useful tool in attaining success. It sets you free, builds healthy relationships, keeps your state of mind at the peak, and increases energy. All these are imperative for success.

Each of us has to account for our own karmas of anger, hatred, and delusion. Forgiveness is an intention with which to approach life. The Bible says, "Forgive, and you shall be forgiven." Take care of your karma, and you will take care of your results.

KARMA 12

Find Your Calling

Finding your calling is going beyond strength and weakness. Merriam-Webster defines a "calling" as "a strong inner impulse toward a particular course of action especially when accompanied by conviction of divine influence." Take a moment each day to focus on the good within you. Then locate the strong impulse that drives you to action. Doing this will help you locate the areas of business that will most advance your success. Finding your calling is essential within your career.

When you find your calling, you will share your true self. We do not always share our true selves. I once asked a friend if there have been times in her professional life that she did not feel she was her true self.

"Oh yes," she said, "This happens most often when I have to give a presentation to a group of vice presidents."

"How does that make you feel?" I inquired further.

"I feel under tremendous pressure and I wait for time to race as quickly as it can," she responded.

I am sure if I were to ask you the same question that I asked her that you too may remember times in your professional life when you did not feel like your true self. I am sure most of us would remember few instances. We work in a world where we are to impress to progress. Last month I delivered a session on "Overcoming the Imposter Syndrome." The room was full of diverse people from various fields of work. As I took the time to get to know my audience, I realized that most were facing the imposter problem. Many admitted that this gives them fear, worry, pressure, and stress. This is because when it comes to being yourself, there can be a lot of pressure from the outside world as it tries to influence you.

I remember Ms. Deepa, the Director of a daycare that I was associated with while at India. She had wonderful skills that were related to curriculum and teaching. She also had an awesome sense of creativity: she could design innovative curriculum that contributed largely to the children's development. Teachers admired her ideas and originality. However, whenever Ms. Deepa would enter the premises, everyone felt a wave of low energy accompanying her. Have you ever met people who are so low that you feel they could really suck the oxygen out from that room? This is how everyone felt when she would enter the school premises.

Ms. Deepa's staff and clients perceived her low energy in their day-to-day interaction with her. At the end of the day when she left the school, a cloud of gloom always remained behind in the daycare. As a director, her role was to keep the team motivated, full of energy, plan out new strategies and ideas, speed up implementation, enhance enrollments, and resolve conflicts. She wasn't able to accomplish any of these things effectively. I witnessed how everyday she dragged herself to work despite her fondness for children and her career.

Years later, I learned that she had moved to another country and was doing exceptionally well in the school she worked at there. She became the head of the curriculum department in a very short time. I wondered how it is possible that the same person does great at one place and poorly at another? When I met her recently, I discovered that the main reason that she did not grow in her earlier job was because she constantly felt under pressure to prove her people management skills to the CEO, to the regional manager, as well as to her staff and clients. She worked hard to enhance her people management skills. Yet, she barely could achieve anything in that area. Everyone seemed to focus on her people management skills. This focus made it difficult for her to concentrate on other aspects of the job. Her energy was so drained trying to work on this area that she lost interest in the curriculum designing.

Her new job gave her a good balance between curriculum design and people management. The people there helped her bring out her creativity and curriculum skills making that her focus area. This helped her build high energy. And as Wayne Dyer said, "Doing what you love is the cornerstone of having abundance in your life." Because she was happy with doing her job, she simultaneously enrolled herself in people management lessons. Today she is the head to the curriculum department.

Today's workplace demands being a peak performer. How can you be a peak performer if your energy is drained impressing others, or working on bringing up skills you either do not possess or aren't good at? How can you motivate someone if your energy is not at its highest peak? If you expect 100 percent energy from your teams, then your expectation from yourself must be 200 percent—always double.

Let me tell you the story of an imaginary rabbit. The rabbit was enrolled in a rabbit school. Like all rabbits, it could hop very well, but could not swim. At the end of the year, the rabbit got high marks in hopping, but failed in swimming. The rabbit's parents were concerned.

"Forget about hopping," the rabbit's parents said, "You are good at that. Concentrate on swimming." Then they sent the rabbit to swimming lessons.

Guess what happened? The rabbit forgot how to hop! As for swimming, have you ever seen a rabbit swim?

Most of us have been raised in an educational system similar to the rabbit's that asks us to focus on limitations and ways to improve. Take my India, my home country, where, like many other places, the schooling system was a fierce competition for the best grades. I remember spending an average of 10–12 h a day studying and doing homework, with barely any time to play. Add to that teachers and parents comparing kids to each other and children scrambling for attention trying to prove themselves as the best. We are taught to follow a line and do what everyone does. All these barely give you a chance to look back on your life and acknowledge all of your achievements.

While it is important for us to know what we are not good at, we must also cherish in the things within which we excel. People are working on their weaknesses and eventually their strengths weaken too. The law of focus says that whatever you hone in on magnifies. Are you magnifying your strengths? It is said, "What comes around goes around." What we learned at school is what we bring to work today. We have become masters in giving attention, time, and energy to all things around us at work, which do not represent our calling.

I oftentimes ask business professionals and corporate managers if they know what their strengths are. Oftentimes, they answer, "Yes." In fact, many companies have online toolkits to identify strengths and weaknesses. Next, I ask them what do they do when they have identified their strengths and weaknesses. They often answer that they work on their weaknesses. They say that they wish to convert their weaknesses to strengths.

But in 8h of work, would you complete meetings, projects, client calls, and targets plus work on your weaknesses? And if your answer is "Yes," then did you get the time to work on your strengths? You need time to enhance the strengths you already possess. Otherwise soon we are all like the rabbit that forgets to hop! Your strength brought you where you are today. It is essential for us to know our weaknesses. But instead of focusing on those weaknesses, learn to convert them into opportunities to magnify your strengths.

When I joined a clothing company as an assistant manager, I would often take work problems to my supervisor. He would sit with me, and we would discuss the options. Many times, he mentioned that I needed to resolve problems on my own and not bring them to his desk. However, resolving problems and being confident about the solution were different experiences for me. After 6 months, when it was time for my first performance appraisal, guess what came up. My problem-solving skills were rated low, and it was an imperative skill to develop for me to be able to continue in this position and grow.

My habit of bringing each and every problem to my supervisor hindered my growth. It was a weakness that I was afraid to work on. As I sat at my desk, I could not think of anything else except how to enhance my problem-solving skills. I spent days and even nights reading books on how to be good at problem-solving. Days turned into weeks, and I became weak in all my other strengths as my concentration was solely on problem-solving skills. Whenever there were team meetings or brainstorming sessions, I put on a mask of confidence that did not help much, but it got me through these meetings. I suffered from imposter syndrome. I was under constant pressure as the next performance appraisal wasn't far.

During this time, the company had organized an event where the CEO was to address all of the staff members. This event greatly changed my life and career. In his speech, the CEO said that each of us must find our calling. We all have a "unique signature power" (USP), something that we are not just good at, but empowered to do. The day you recognize your USP and work on enhancing it will be the day that you become an unstoppable leader. He urged us to find our calling.

That night I could not sleep. His words kept echoing in my mind. The next day I decided to stop battling with being a great problem solver—it was not in me. But at the same time, I did not ignore the problem. I decided to find my calling and use that to convert my weakness into strength. My true calling was giving advice and coaching. I was known among my team and peers as someone they could come to for advice and coaching.

I decided to use this to help me be a better problem solver, if not the best at that time. So now whenever there was a problem, I would go to my supervisor (old habits die hard!). But I would go with two recommendations on how we could possibly solve the problem. I would also present a coaching style that asked and answered questions that led to deeper thinking. This helped me at that time to improve on my problem-solving skills. It also connected me to my true calling, which is coaching and guiding people on the path to their success.

You did not enter the workforce to just be pushed to another grade level or get another client. You entered the workforce to make a difference, to become unique, like no one else. Strive to make a difference in your career, no matter how small. Don't bury that calling under the daily grind of work life. There is within us a strong inner impulse toward a particular course of action and when you find that calling and act on it, it will determine how successful you are in your professional life. Become the best possible that YOU can be. The day you unleash yourself and reach to that person within you and find your calling, that day you will be unstoppable!

Many people are in search of their purpose or true calling in their career lives. Just because we have callings doesn't mean they're easy to follow. We need to dig in deep and try out various options and, most importantly, hear our inner voice in silence. That is when we find the true calling that liberates yourself from the cycle of work–life balance. Everything will appear in harmony. Accentuate what is best within you with these three simple steps.

- **Step 1**—Become aware: The first thing is to become aware of your calling. Ask yourself this: what is it that you are really good at? We are all born with, or have developed, talents and strengths that distinguish us from those around us. Can you think of three things you do better than most other people do? Is it managing people, doing finance, coaching, mentoring, or repairing machines? Whatever it is, you must become truly aware of it.
- **Step 2**—Develop focus: Now that you are aware of your true calling, focus on it. Let your focus grow. You want to grow your positive strengths. When you focus on what matters most, you find yourself surrounded with possibilities. It wires your brain to look for the best.
- **Step 3**—Build habits: Humans are creatures of habit. You want to build new habits to strengthen your calling. Set aside at least 30 min daily to support your calling. This is when creating the space within your life for your strengths will be important. Daily small steps will help you fulfill your calling.

As you read this, I urge you today to find your calling. This is not about just wanting to do something different. It is about living to your full potential and discovering what you are truly best at. There is something within each of you that will take you to the next level of your career. Only you are aware of this. Each of us has a unique signature power that will help us grow. Become what you are. Don't become someone else. The professional world doesn't need that. Don't get lost in the crowd of people aiming at becoming just another rabbit who forgot to hop.

Your calling will change with time, environment, and age. Every 5 years, look back and edit your calling to learn from the old and see what's new. But remember at all times that there is something in you that will constantly tell you that you can do more. Hear that voice. Create what you want. Your career will put pressures and demands on you. If you hold your head up, and follow your calling, then you will achieve success.

KARMA 13

Be Unstoppable

Everyday work stressors can wear you down. Yet, despite the stress, you've got to achieve your career goals. You've got to make it there. If you want to be successful, then it is time to wake up and be the unstoppable business person that you are destined to be. Businesses spend an enormous amount of money on trainings that will help their leaders and teams to be more productive and engaged at work. But the results still fall short. Statistics show that more than half of the people at work are disengaged. The best of us possess endurance, unshakeable faith, insane patience, and a bounce-back attitude so strong that no one can defeat you. You must be the best. You must be unstoppable.

Our careers will be turbulent. There will be peaks and valleys. How were we able to be resilient in the face of failure and criticism when we were children? Look back at your life and you will see that you were unbreakable and unstoppable as a youth. You had to be so that you could grow into adulthood. Yet, oftentimes as an adult, you let roadblocks stop your progress toward success. This is because as we age, many of us become even more fearful within our professional lives. That fear causes pain.

Pain is inevitable. Sometimes it arises because of the people within our professional lives. Other times it arises because of the circumstances. But remember what is painful to you may be pleasurable for someone else. Pain and pleasure are everywhere, and they often come in cycles. Your loss is someone's gain. So pain and pleasure are illusions. Our mind converts an event into pain or pleasure. If your mind perceives an event or behavior as painful, then your energy level drops, and your emotions become disturbed. Your thoughts and energy are depleted in working toward eradicating that pain. With this state of mind, you aren't able to make beneficial decisions and take correct actions for growth and success.

Most people don't advance in their careers because of fear of this pain. I am talking about the pain of rejection, defeat, sadness, failure, or judgment. I know many business owners who could not expand their business as much as they wished to because of a crippling fear of failure. I know corporate leaders who got stuck at the grade level they were in because of a painful fear of leaving their comfort zone. Most people stay close to the ground where it is safe instead of soaring in their careers.

When a child is born, the mother and child both go through pain. The caterpillar struggles inside a cocoon to flex its wings as it becomes a butterfly. Every pain has a pleasure attached to it. Find that pleasure, and the pain will be bearable. If you keep moving ahead you will get there. Persist until you succeed. It takes time to grow your business, your career, and yourself.

Just like a Chinese bamboo tree in its first year, we see no visible signs of activity and growth. In the second year, again, we see no growth above the soil. The third, the fourth: still we see nothing. Finally, in the fifth year, we experience growth. And what growth it is! The Chinese bamboo tree grows 80 ft in just 6 weeks. It's not the 6 weeks, but the 5 years that lead to exponential growth. It takes time to grow the unseen roots to get the fruits. People who patiently work toward their dreams and goals, and who overcome obstacles, will grow the strong internal foundation toward unstoppable success.

When things at work are hard, when you are going through pain, when everything seems overwhelming, when there seems to be no growth, and when things seem to be moving backward instead of forward—when any of these things are true, say to yourself with full conviction: "This too shall pass." Repeat it with me now: this too shall pass.

What matters most is how you overcome pain and defeat. Unstoppable success means you need to be unbroken. You must be unbroken by circumstances, people, and events. You must be unbroken by your own emotions. For me there are three pillars of unstoppable success within our careers:

- Unshakeable faith in self and in the higher power.
- Incredible patience to bear whatever comes your way.
- Bounce-back attitude to get back on track quickly.

Without these pillars, there is no unstoppable success. When you realize these pillars, you achieve a successful mindset: a mind with full faith, patience, and persistence, and a mind that is willing to bounce back and stay busy. We live in a quick-fix society. We want instant solutions to every complex problem and every fractured relationship. Pursuing your dream is a sure thing if you just don't give up. So long as you keep watering and fertilizing your dream, it will come to fruition, just like the Chinese bamboo tree. It may take weeks. It may take months. It may even take years. But eventually, the roots will take hold and, like the Chinese bamboo tree, they will grow exponentially.

If the foundation is strong, then the pillars will be able to withstand any pressure and force. That foundation is you—your mind. It needs to be stable and undisturbed as much as possible. There are two places that require our endurance within our professional lives. One is the external endurance toward people and situations at work, and the other is internal endurance, our inner mindset.

There are many books that help achieve healthy workplace relationships and ultimately higher productivity in our jobs. Yet, how successful are we? Many times we face problems at work with the behaviors of peers, clients, bosses, or teams. Day-to-day routine situations and behaviors may irritate us and makes us angry. Yet, even when we may be irritated and angry, we must continue to make decisions, motivate people, influence others, and build healthy relationships with clients.

Doing this requires endurance. Endurance is the foundation of unstoppable success on which the pillars are based. Endurance is the ability to push through wear and tear and still complete the task at hand. We are all fairly familiar with how to build physical endurance. But we may not understand how to build the kind of strong mental and emotional endurance that leads to unstoppable success. Those who possess this trait can persevere when times get tough and those without it will fold up shop and go home. Many of us feel that our careers are like long journeys or battlefields typified by tough competition. Whatever is your view of your career, you are in it now. Thus, it is imperative that you become a winner. You will never know the obstacles and benefits that await you. You must depend on yourself the most. No one will stop her or his journey for you. You must pick yourself up and bounce back quickly. It really does not matter how you started. It only matters how you finish. So finish strong.

I once coached a 61-year-old, energetic lady who was appointed the Director of a nonprofit business center. I was amazed by her commitment and her never-give-up attitude at this golden age. She faced numerous challenges with her staff who felt that it was difficult to relate with her due to her physical limitations. But she decided that she would take up the challenge and finish strong.

Here's another example of a business leader who understood the value of endurance. Brad Cohen is a motivational speaker, teacher, school administrator, and author who suffered from severe Tourette's syndrome. During his childhood, Cohen endured a difficult childhood and numerous frustrations even as an adult because of the Tourette's syndrome. He decided to become the teacher that he never had. After he graduated and received his teaching certificate, 24 elementary schools rejected him before he was hired at Cobb County Elementary School in Georgia. As a new teacher, he experienced many challenges but decided to never give up. He later received the 1997 Sallie Mae First Class Teacher of the Year award. Since then he has accomplished many heights in his career.

Here's another example: Chris Gardner is an American businessman, investor, stockbroker, motivational speaker, author, and philanthropist, who, during the 1980s, struggled with homelessness while raising his toddler son. In 1987, Gardner established the brokerage firm, Gardner Rich & Co. He wrote a best-selling memoir called *The Pursuit of Happyness* that is a testament to his endurance as a business leader. His book was turned into a movie starring Will Smith.

These are real people with high mental endurance who decided to finish strong. How much wear and tear can you take on your journey to unstoppable success? The only way to truly gain high endurance is to train, to practice, and to keep moving ahead. The unstoppable success of these great leaders reminds me of a poem that the great American poet Henry Wadsworth Longfellow wrote about another wise figure in history, "The Ladder of Saint Augustine." Saint Augustine of Hippo was one of the giants of early Christianity who turned a life of suffering into pioneering church reformation. He is one of the few people to be recognized as a saint in all three of the major Christian traditions: Catholicism, Eastern Orthodox, and Anglican Communion. In the poem, Wadsworth says the following about Saint Augustine:

> The heights by great men reached and kept
> Were not attained by sudden flight,
> But they, while their companions slept,
> Toiled ever upward through the night.

At an early age, I witnessed an incident that inspired me. My father and I were taking a stroll in the garden. I was in the early years of my career, and I was slightly disturbed by an incident that took place at work. I was facing conflicts with some members in the management team because of my young age, and I wasn't taken seriously enough as the Human Resource Manager. It seemed as if every day they were ready to throw imaginary bricks at my team and me. I knew my potential and that I could achieve much in my position. But irritation and anger consumed me.

For weeks at stretch, I was enduring both the management's behavior and the disturbances within my own inner environment.

On our walk through the garden, my dad stopped near a mango tree, which was laden with fruit. He started throwing stones at the tree until a few mangoes rained down on us.

"Isn't it impressive that after I threw stones at the tree, the tree gave us sweet fruit in return," said my father as we enjoyed the sweet fruit. Then he continued, saying, "In winter when people will chop trees down to arrange logs for fire, even after being chopped and burnt, the tree will continue giving warmth to the people. It doesn't matter what people throw at you. All that matters is what you make out of it and give in return."

That day I learned a lifelong professional lesson: if someone throws stones at you, you give them fruits in return. I returned to work the next day determined to give my best even if it seemed that stones were thrown at me. I knew I had to quit the feelings of irritation and anger within me. I did not have to endure the management's behavior. All I had to do was to take proper action. I had passion, vigor, knowledge, and positivity to give. Eventually things got better, and the resentment died down.

Take a moment to reflect on this and ask yourself this: when stones are being thrown at you in your workplace, what do you give back? You can only give what you have internalized. If you have been enduring bitterness, resentment, jealousy, doubts, then that is what you will give back. But if you have internalized happiness, acceptance, and determination, then that is what you will give back. In the business and corporate world, stones are thrown. There will be dirty politics, backstabbing, competition, and resentment. Yet what you do with these stones will determine your future. Do you allow these obstacles to hurt you or do you build a foundation of success despite the challenges? This will largely depend on your inner dialogue. Pay attention to how you talk back to yourself within your mind. Keep telling yourself to get rid of fear, stress, a sense of failure, anxiety, past hurts, anger, resentment, negativity, and doubt.

During one of my coaching sessions, a business owner often mentioned his frustration with the emails that he received from his Russian clients. Whenever he would send emails to them, they would call him up to speak about the details, which he had already articulated in his original email. The business owner said that this took away from his schedule and made him question why he sent the original email in the first place. He simply could not understand why they called to speak to him about every single detail from the email. It turned out that, while American businesspeople do much of their business by written communication like email, many Russian professionals still prefer to hear things directly from people they trust. Phone or face-to-face meetings are usually more productive for them. The businessman's impatience and irritation stopped him from understanding the cross-cultural differences of his client. I worked with him on quieting the irritation within his mind so that he could become unstoppable again.

Incidents like these stop us from soaring in our professional lives. We spiral downward, feeling annoyed, and drained out. If we get tired and put off by these daily incidents at work, what stamina do we have remaining to endure greater challenges as we work to become unstoppable? Even the smallest challenges will test your tenacity. But you must build an uncomplaining endurance to keep moving forward. The businessman needed a congenial perspective to endure and accept his clients' cultural differences. So too will you need mental endurance when dealing with your teams, with your clients, and with all of the people with whom you engage within your professional life. People who refuse to remain complacent in good times, who keep pushing themselves, and who are agile and resilient are the ones that stay in the professional race and win.

Let me close this reflection on being unstoppable with one more example from the life of a successful leader. When he was experimenting with the electric bulb, Thomas Edison, the pioneering American inventor, was looking for an appropriate filament. He and his team tested and tried nearly 6,000 possible materials. Ultimately, carbonized bamboo proved to be suitable element to be used a filament for electric bulb. It requires great mental strength to experiment with so many elements. Not only does it require skill, but it also requires an attitude of uncomplaining endurance.

With the endurance of Edison and other pioneers in mind, I often suggest a technique called the "5 Minute Alarm" to my clients. When you are attacked by emotions and thoughts that disturb you, the 5 Minute Alarm gets you out of a negative internal state quickly. Many of my clients mentioned that, at first, it was tough to move their emotions and thoughts out of a negative state in just 5 min because their body and mind were tuned to stay in a disturbed state for long period of time. Giving yourself a time limit to breathe deeply and snap out of negative thinking is like an alarm clock ringing us awake. We push the "snooze" button to get five more minutes of sleep. But then the alarm tells us again that we must snap out of our slumber and rise to our challenges.

Today, most of my clients no longer need the image of the 5 Minute Alarm to help them as they stop their negative thinking. Their body and mind have become unstoppable automatically. We all go through difficult situations and encounter difficult people. But ultimately, it is your internal adjustments within your mind that will help you renew productive energy. You are a powerhouse of energy. Your positivity is like a magnet that attracts success. Keep your focus on the things that you want to do without distractions. Be unstoppable!

KARMA 14

Be Your Own Role Model

I am sometimes invited to offer motivational presentations before entrepreneurs. When I ask my audience to share with me who their role model is, some say it is an athlete, a business leader, their peer, their boss, or any other famous personality. Surprisingly, no one offers his or her own name as a role model. I realized then and now the importance of being our own role model. Look up to yourself. Learn from yourself. Better yourself each day.

In fact, do you remember being asked to write a paper in high school about who you look up to and why? We were conditioned to believe that someone outside of us should be looked up to. And today, we have become habituated to consider ourselves to be anything but the best. Buddha said, "You can search throughout the entire universe for someone who is more deserving of your love and affection than you are yourself, and that person is not to be found anywhere. You, yourself, as much as anybody in the entire universe, deserve your love and affection." Think about it. Do you make things happen? Are you aware of what you want? Do you know how to get what you want? Do you work diligently? Do you demonstrate confidence? Do you show respect for your clients, boss, peers, and people? Do you fulfill your commitments? Have you overcome obstacles? Are you humble? Do you stay positive most of the days? Do you achieve most of your goals?

If you answered yes to most of the questions, you are the best role model for yourself. A role model is someone you look up to, and someone from whom you learn. Don't you look up to yourself? Don't you learn from your mistakes and achievements? Are you not an achiever? Maybe it sounds overconfident when you say that you are your own role model, but that's okay. You have overcome your share of obstacles along the way, and have been moving ahead. You have your strengths and weakness just like anyone else. So, when you write about role model, your name must be at the top of the list among others. The problem is, we are so consumed in our daily to-do lists that we have forgotten that there is a role model within us that is getting crushed under criticism and negativity of the daily routine.

If you meet someone who keeps talking to you about their failures, flaws, and weaknesses, would you consider them as your role model? Chances are you said no. Now look at how many times in a day you remind yourself about your weaknesses, failures, and flaws. We feel uplifted when someone tells us that we have many good qualities. But we are unable to see our own good qualities. So the search for a role model starts outside. We are role models for others and others are role models for us. But barely anyone considers their own self as a role model for themselves. When the person we look up to achieves something we say to ourselves, "s/he had to achieve, s/he is an achiever." How many times have you repeated this sentence to yourself when you take up an assignment or achieve something? Have you constantly reminded yourself that you are an achiever, and you are successful? We barely remind our self about this fact of our life. We praise others but criticize our self.

When Barbara, a client, desperately wanted to start her own hiring consultancy business, she worked tirelessly in the formative years. She perceived people around her were successful in their start-up but she wasn't. Every time she saw this, she criticized herself and felt she was no good. This self-criticism created a broken relation with herself. Her passion for business subsided, tension loomed over her, and she was in debt and soon gave up. She later took up a full-time job. Every day at work there are many situations you face where you criticize yourself. When you criticize yourself continuously, you have a broken relation with your own self. Every day you make sure to motivate your teams, you are careful with words you use with others.

However, in a day you spend most of your time with yourself. And what you speak to yourself about yourself is very important. That's the imprint you leave on your mind. I have coached numerous people, and I observed that unknowingly they often say to me and to themselves phrases like, "I get angry very easily" or "I cannot achieve what he achieved" or "I am not ready to take on a big client" or "I am stressed out." Now the more you repeat phrases like these to yourself, the more you create a strong imprint on your mind about it. It now becomes your habit to get angry, to feel stressed on little things. And with a habit like this how much can you achieve? Today we look for role models outside because inside us there is someone who has been crushed under self-criticism.

Here's a thoughtful Tibetan story I had heard and that I share in my seminars. It was about a rich king who had four wives. The king loved his fourth wife the most and adorned her with riches. He also loved his third wife and was always showing her off to neighboring kingdoms. However, he always feared that she would leave him. His second wife was kind, considerate, and his trusted confidante in difficult times. Wife number one was devoted and loyal and although she loved him deeply, he was not as interested and tended to ignore her.

One day, the king fell ill and the truth dawned that his life was soon to end. He thought of the luxurious life he had led and feared being alone when he died.

"I have loved you the most," he tells his fourth wife, "endowed you with the finest clothing, showered gifts upon you and taken great care over you. Now that I'm dying, will you follow me and keep me company?"

"No way!" she replied and walked away without another word.

The sad king then asked the third wife:

"I have loved you all my life. Now that I'm dying, will you follow me and keep me company?"

"No!" she replied. "Life is too good! When you die, I'm going to remarry!"

He then asked the second wife:

"I have always turned to you for help and you've always been there for me. When I die, will you follow me and keep me company?"

"I'm sorry, I can't help you out this time!" she replied. "At the very most, I can help with your funeral."

Then a voice called out to the king in his sadness:

"I'll leave with you and follow you no matter where you go." The king looked up, and there was his first wife. She was so skinny and undernourished. Greatly grieved, the king said:

"I should have taken much better care of you when I had the chance!"

In reality, we all have four wives in our careers. Our fourth wife is our skill. We invest a lot of money, time, and effort in enhancing it, though it'll leave us when we retire. Our third wife is our role, title, and position. We get attached to these but when we retire, it will all go to others. Someone new will fill in for us. Our second wife is our teams, management, people, clients, and office friends. We put in all the efforts to be good with them and to build relationship. No matter how much they have supported and loved us, they will not be with us forever.

Our first wife is our mind, our own self: often neglected in pursuit of career ladder, wealth, power, growth, and competition. However, our mind is the only thing that will follow us wherever we go. Care for your skill set and keep it up to date so you can keep progressing to the fullest. Enjoy your titles and wealth. Cherish your team, your people, and your clients. But don't forget to nourish your mind as it is the source of all your life and will prove to be your most faithful friend. Take care of yourself if you truly must be a role model to yourself and others. It appears somewhat confusing but to be your own role model is a brilliant idea because it is the basis of everything—relationships, creative expression, and growth. It shows you value self.

On your journey to success if there is someone who would stay with you until the end it's you. People will meet you on the way, some may even accompany you, but no one will finish the journey with you except you yourself. I agree that we must look up to certain people as a role model as that acts as a guide on our journey. However, we must aspire to be our own role model. You must learn from your mistakes instead of getting into self-criticism. You must speak assertively to yourself just like you do with others.

You must be careful in choosing the words when you talk to yourself. Nonacceptance and blaming circumstances and people make you feel like a victim. Once you feel like a victim your energy is depleted. What is the quality of your actions and results now? Think about it. When your team comes to you feeling low or upset, what do you say to them. Do you say, "hey no worries, it will be all okay." Do you try honestly to uplift the spirits? Now ask the same question to yourself that when you feel upset or low, do you say to yourself, "Hey no worries, it will be all okay." Do you try honesty to uplift your spirits? Even when everyone around you criticizes you, your quality or your work doesn't immediately start to criticize yourself. Analyze and then move ahead. You will meet many people who will pull you down, criticize you, or help you. They will all enter and exit your journey, but if you are your own role model you will always look up to yourself, you will depend most on yourself, and you will stay with yourself until the end of the journey. No situation will be able to disturb your state of mind. If your state of mind is healthy, you will have positive energy to take action and achieve your results.

The reason I encourage my clients and my readers to be their own role model is because no one can help you to get where you want to accept yourself. No one knows you better than yourself. Your deepest secrets, weaknesses, and strengths are known to you alone. You know your blueprint better than anyone. Inspire yourself to become better at what you do. We usually wait for someone to recognize our work, to give us a pat on the back, to tell us we are doing great, to motivate us. It makes us feel so good when others appreciate us. But people do not always have the time to appreciate. It may be once in a while that your boss comes up to you and says you are doing a super job. Or a client emails you about how happy they are with your services. No doubt, having a role model and being appreciated is a part of our work life, and it makes us feel good. However, let that flow in whenever it does. But on a day to day basis be your own role model.

The essence of a role model is that they have qualities like they lead by setting examples, are a source of inspiration, they inspire others even in the times of hardship, they have the strength to tread the unexplored paths, they are always at peace, very loving, and sensitive, they learn from their triumphs and mistake, they respect self and others, they have a never give up attitude, they have an open mind, they are passionate about whatever they do, they finish whatever they have started, they believe in self, and they listen to their inner voice.

Look within yourself, you will definitely find the person with all these qualities. Embrace your experience. Be a role model to self-first so you can be a role model to others. In the spirit in which you are happy, positive, joyful, passionate, full of belief, focused on the right thing, you are the hero of your career life. In the spirit in which you are angry, stressed, distracted, doubtful, worrying, you are the anti-hero of your career life.

KARMA 15

Decode the Message

Have you ever wondered why some things at work keep happening in the same way all the time? Have you ever wondered how an impossible deal suddenly came through? Has it happened that you were next in line to get a salary hike, but for no reason the company suddenly stopped salary hike for that year? Have you ever turned on the radio and heard a song that speaks directly to your current circumstances that just happens to be playing? Think of it this way: There are no coincidences. To everything there is a reason and a season. The universe sends you a message in every event that happens in your careers. You must decode the message to achieve success.

A couple of years back, I remember reading about the cockroach theory by Sundar Pichai, the CEO of Google, Inc. The article is based on a story of what happened in a restaurant. A cockroach landed on one of the ladies in a group of diners. She immediately screams and tries to rid herself of the cockroach. The cockroach jumps from one person to the next, and the others panic too. A waiter comes to the group's rescue. Despite the fact that the cockroach also managed to land on the waiter's shirt, his reaction was different. Instead of screaming, he stood composed: he observed the cockroach's behavior and then calmly caught it and threw it out the door.

Sipping my coffee and reading this article several years ago, I wondered if it was the cockroach that was responsible for the diners' panic. If so, then why was the waiter not disturbed? The truth of the matter is that the problem is not the cockroach. The problem is the inability of those people to handle the disturbance caused by the cockroach. Similarly, it is not the situation or the people that disturbs us, but our inability to handle the disturbances caused by the situations that actually disturb us.

The problem is that we have buried ourselves in our daily work that we don't pay attention to these hidden messages. Many of us feel that hard-to-explain events have no meaning at all in our professional lives. Though our seemingly inexplicable situations may be similar, their impact is different for each of us. For some, it is a matter of what we left undone in the past and now the unexplained event is actually the completion of a karmic cycle.

What do I mean when I say the "universe"? Quantum physics shows us that everything in our universe is energy. Furthermore, everything in the universe has its own energy level. Even our thoughts are energy vibrating. Whatever thoughts we choose, they vibrate at a certain frequency that attracts elements that vibrate at the same frequency. That is why the saying "like attracts like" is important. So the more you discuss that ill-tempered boss, that discontented team member, that annoying customer, then the more you attract these people to you. In short, the more you discuss your problems the more of them you attract. You must learn to analyze and direct the energies around you.

Success and prosperity are not purely because of hard work and skillset. Many people who have made it big in their field of expertise continually say a common phrase: I followed my gut. Do these words sound familiar to you? Following your gut is the same as decoding the message the universe gives you. Your gut feeling becomes stronger when you pay attention to it. How many times have you taken these intuitive messages and decoded them? When your boss and you have conflicts; when growth is stuck despite all your efforts; when you get new clients sooner than others; when business starts to flourish suddenly; when every job you take up leads to failures; when any of these things happen, your gut is speaking to you. You must listen, pinpoint, the larger meaning of these situations, and then discern what they mean to you.

Rather than decoding the message, we fixate on the problems. Fixating on problems is the biggest problem of all. You must attune your mind to believe that the problems that you have are not problems at all. Obsessing over problems is the biggest problem of all. More than the problem, it's your reaction to the problem that creates chaos in your professional life. When a particular situation comes your way, your mind decides if it is a problem or not. Many problems are fictitious.

What appears a problem to you is a blessing to another. Let's take, for example, the case of two business partners. These men formed a partnership in a security systems business. Business started to grow well and profits poured in. After a couple of years, with the onset of digital security, their technology needed upgrades, and their business faced a loss. One of the partners could not endure the loss and suffered a heart attack. The other accepted the problem, endured the loss, analyzed further steps to address the issue, and moved on: same situation, but different responses.

Have you ever wondered why two people respond differently to the same conflict? One is disturbed and the other is calm. One feels hopeless and the other is full of hope. The reason lies in the art of decoding. How you analyze or interpret a situation or person goes a long way to deciding the success of your professional life. Now this does not mean that all problems will be solved completely all the time. It is much beyond this. This is about the art of decoding messages that universe gives you in the form of events, problems, achievements, and people. Every event that comes to you, every person who comes your way represents a reason and a season.

Let me ask you this: is corporate life any different from those who are in the arena of sports or cinema? If people in these sports and the cinema are able to decode messages for their success, then why not people in business? We all have the right to be as successful as we want to be. The only thing needed is to stretch ourselves beyond skills and conditions as we tune our minds to success. If you stop for a moment— just a moment—and listen closely, really looking at the subtle signs, what do you hear?

Often our days are so packed with to-do lists that we completely ignore the message. This is why we undergo stress, illness, and anxiety when things go the other way in our professional life. We get so deeply engrossed in the "why" that we can't take a step back and decode the message.

Ask yourself this: what's in it for me? What is the universe trying to tell me through this incident or person? I can almost assure you that when you step back to decode the message you will move forward with double energy and force. Just like the arrow must be pulled back before it shoots out to the target, you must take a step back to decode the messages the universe sends you.

Our best trainings in communication aren't teaching us how to communicate with the biggest source of your success: the Universe. My dad would always read Vedic scriptures to me, and one thing that the scripture stated was that the universe communicates through events and people that enter and exit our life. Every event and every person exists for a reason and a season. That is why no one stays around you permanently: every event and every person that relates to you is temporary. Your success depends on how quickly you decode the message while they are with you.

In my career, there have been numerous incidences where I observed the universe giving me messages. Many of these I ignored and many I decoded. The messages I ignored got louder. The universe will keep bringing the message to you until it gets your attention. For example, you are frustrated with your job and wish you could join another company, but you aren't getting enough confidence to do so. You may notice that you keep bumping into a certain person from another company, or a job posting repeatedly comes in front of you. And one day you take the action and you get into your new job.

Now let me share with you three true stories about people who faced the challenge of decoding the messages that the universe told them. Two of the stories are about my clients, and the other is a familiar tale of a man whose family escaped likely death aboard the Titanic.

Rachel, the Motivational Speaker

Rachel was a client of mine who worked in Human Resources as a generalist. She was passionate about her job. She was smart, hardworking, and she seemed to be climbing the corporate ladder to success sooner than expected. However, she was never able to stick in one job for more than 2 years. Either nature would remove her from the job or her own personal circumstances would intrude. This frustrated her a lot, and she continued from one job to another with periods of transition for almost 15 years.

During periods of transitions she would often get offers to volunteer for free trainings on Human Resources policies and customer service. People loved her way of speaking. But as soon as she would find a job, she would go back to it. Every time she asked herself why is this happening to me—why was there "bad luck" in her career? It wasn't until 2014 when nature pushed her out of her last job as a Human Resources Training Head that she took a step back to decode it all.

She decided to do something in the field of public speaking. She worked hard and smart, and this time results were in her favor. And as luck would have it, today she is a successful motivational speaker. When she looks back, she always wishes that she had paid close attention to the message the universe was giving her when it did not let her settle down in one job. She would have saved herself from the roller coaster ride of emotions and frustration. What she considered "bad luck" was actually the universe directing her to her path of success.

Mark, the Global Businessman

Now let me tell you about Mark a French businessman who lived in America. He had a great American job along with a loving family. But he often expressed a desire to return back to his home in France to be close to his parents. He took the leap. He spoke with his company and requested a re-location. The company said things looked good, and they could relocate him to the company branch office in France. He put his home for sale, started to sell off his goods that could not be shipped, and was getting ready to move. But then he got the email from his company's management that due to economic policy changes in America all international moves were being placed on a hold, including international job openings.

By then Mark had sold his home, and his goods were at the dock ready to be shipped. He still went ahead with the move by letting his family go back to France and told them that he would follow after few months. However, all of a sudden, the company's market value hits a downward spiral, and he could not take the move to France. He had to call his family back to America and resettle.

He agreed that the universe had given him many signs and messages to not go ahead with the move, but he hadn't decoded them. This led to losses in his personal and professional life. Of course, today he is doing well and is finally in France at a great post. He now makes sure he decodes the message from the universe and uses it to become successful and prosperous.

Mr. Clark and the *Titanic*

A Scottish gentleman named Mr. Clark made plans for his wife and nine children to travel to the United States aboard the *Titanic* in 1912. It took many years to save up enough money for the whole family to board the new ocean liner and sail to America. The entire family was filled with anticipation and excitement about their new life.

However, 7 days before their departure, a dog bit the youngest son. The doctor sewed up the boy, but hung a yellow sheet on the Clark family's front door to notify the public of a possible rabies infection. Subsequently, the entire family was quarantined and barred from leaving the country for 14 days. The father went to the dock to watch the *Titanic* sail away without him and his family, and he cursed everyone for what seemed like his misfortune.

Yet, his curses turned to exaltations 5 days later after the "unsinkable" ship sank when he learned that his family had escaped the tragedy that unfolded after the *Titanic* hit an iceberg, and most of the passengers drowned. The universe was talking to the Clark family, and it took a quarantine to force them to listen.

So you got laid off. Your business is going down. Orders have been canceled. An economic downturn has come. Although we may not always understand, all things of these things happen for a reason. Problems and opportunities are so relative. Something that seems a problem turns out to be good in the course of the time. The intention of the Universe is pure. It wants each of us to succeed and fulfill our dreams. It has great plans for you, for me, and for everyone who desires to achieve. Let's not get in our own way by cursing the situation or the universe like Mr. Clark did.

Rejection is one big sign that the universe has something bigger and better for us. It is also a sign that your efforts will be double than what they are now. However, we consider rejection as a sign that it's over, a dead end. Most of us decode the universe's message in the other way and enter the wrong way zone. The universe will bring you back on the right path and will keep holding your hand until you get the message and reach your destination.

At every step in your career life the universe provides you with enough subtle signs to help you decide if you should continue along the path or ditch it completely. Pay attention to these messages, and they'll reveal when it's time to let go and move on. I often give my clients what I call the SAT technique.

Silence: Take a step back and be in silence. In silence, your mind slows down and you will be able to hear the universe. Tell the universe your doubt, your problem, and your goal, and ask it to help by revealing the next steps.

Awareness: The next step is to focus on increasing your ability to spot patterns and recurring experiences or events. Become aware of what patterns the universe has been sending you. Be aware of your feelings and experiences.

Trust: When the student is ready, the teacher will appear. Trust in the message that you get from the universe, trust the source, and trust yourself. Don't come in your own way by resisting the message you get or fighting to know more. Just be receptive and trust.

Another powerful technique is called POQ: Power of Questions. Most of the time we are caught in the web of the why and the when of the problems in our professional lives, and this disturbs out state of mind. To decode the message of the universe, ask questions that focus on the solution rather than the problem itself:

- How can I make this work?
- What can I do to help change this?
- How can I use this for learning?
- How do I navigate my way ahead?

Today I challenge you to listen. Don't wait for the message to hit you over the head. In the words of Abraham Hicks: "The entire universe is conspiring to give you everything you want." Take a step back and think about what message have you been ignoring. The universe is here to serve you and take you to your destination. Everyone is born to be successful. You have success within you. The universe will do everything to get you there. You must be ready to listen and decode the message.

KARMA 16

Believe Anew

All of our actions are based on our beliefs. If you believe a certain thing cannot be done, then it will not be done. You will find all excuses for not doing the thing even if it is possible. On the other hand, if there is a task that seems impossible to achieve, and you believe it can be done, then you will do everything to achieve. Success is a vehicle. It moves on the wheel of hard work and fuel of self-belief. The message you give to yourself is the message that comes back to you in the form of your results. Manage your beliefs and you'll better manage your results.

At work in past years, I would always connect and motivate my teams. Yet, I would still hear from some that they felt unappreciated. It pained me to see that my efforts weren't delivering the expected results expected. Soon I formed a belief that doing anything extra is no good and one should do just enough. Of course, this belief did me no good, and it clouded my thinking. It's our beliefs that guide us toward or away from our goals.

Here's another example of a problematic belief. Over the past few decades, I've worked with hundreds of people, and many complain that they work for micromanagers. Many leaders micromanage because they believe that people cannot be trusted and that micromanagement gives them power and control. Doubt hinders progress. While it is a good practice to pause and question yourself to determine loophole in the project, doubting yourself or people is not a good practice.

We form many beliefs each day at work. They're formed by our knowledge, environment, habits, and influence of peers, past experiences, pain, and happiness. Once formed, these beliefs become ingrained in us. Have you ever noticed that multiple people consider the same boss, peer, client, project, or meetings differently? This is because each of us at work has our own set of beliefs. So when we interact with people, we are actually interacting with their belief. A belief is like a map that each of us carries with us. With this map we understand and navigate our careers. Many times our maps are different from others and if we do not appreciate each other's maps, conflicts at the workplace arise.

Most of our beliefs are limiting: they cause us to miss out on the things that we want most. Think about a goal that you absolutely want to achieve. Now think about some of your beliefs associated with that goal. Are your beliefs about your goal optimistic or pessimistic? Are they connecting you to your goals or disconnecting you? Do they empower you or disempower you? Are they stopping you or driving you toward unstoppable success? It is very important to know what your belief is doing for you.

I have met numerous business and corporate leaders who have told me that tension at work is natural. This belief that tension is natural makes them insensitive toward it. Then their attitude and their actions are filled with tension. Soon they have tension-related physical issues. Many business articles describe the prevalence of early heart attacks and other physical ailments that people encounter during their careers. Often this is not because of their workload. It's because of their unshakeable, problematic belief that tension is the only solution to getting anything done at work.

A client of mine from the healthcare industry was facing tough market competition. They were making internal and external changes to approach the market in a new way. The changes involved downsizing as well updating their product line. I was hired to coach and offer workshops to their managers and team. I was told that the teams are not motivated for this change. So before the workshop, my team and I conducted prefatory one-on-one sessions with the teams. This gave us an indication that the teams were not confident about the change and the reasons they shared were ambiguous.

I further conducted a one-on-one with the managers and this is where I got clarity. Out of the 19 managers, who were from different departments, I clearly remember that 14 of them did not believe that change was possible. None of these managers had shared those beliefs directly with any of their team members. They were motivating their teams toward this change and sharing and giving them a bright vision.

At the same time, they did not believe in what they were sharing with their teams. Their teams unconsciously picked up on their manager's divided purpose. The team then became unconfident about the change. How did they feel what their managers felt? Your teams are not only affected by the message. The messenger also affects them. The best of the speech, reports, and emails will do no good if your belief is infested with doubt. This is because every email you send or interaction you have with the team will vibrate with that doubt regardless of what you say. And this is what was happening with these managers and their teams.

We are all continuously radiating a vibration. What that vibration is depends on our predominant thoughts and emotions in any given moment. These moment-by-moment beliefs have a massive impact on your actions. If your thoughts are full of doubts, negativity, or unhappiness, then that doubt will vibrate through your communication and body language. This is why even the best speech, emails, and actions will do no good if your beliefs are disjointed. Quantum physics says that atoms work purely through vibrating energy waves. Humans are made up of atoms that are continuously emitting and absorbing energy. Each atom has its own distinct frequency or vibration. It helps to visualize that whatever your frequency will be the frequency of those around you. If you wonder why your team is not passionate, why negative people at work, why you are not getting potential clients, surround you then the answer lies within you. Be conscious of your vibrations. Look at your beliefs and discover their frequency. Adjust your mind to get what you want.

Yet, another client of mine landed his dream job at a Fortune 500 company and was very excited about it. But once he started in the new role, things started to go downhill. He was hearing feedback that he wasn't playing a leadership role and not speaking up enough at team meetings. When I explored his problem together, my client confessed. "I don't want my ideas to be judged. Everyone in the room is smart." Underlying his behavior was the belief that others were smarter than he was. This is a classic example of a limiting belief. This limiting belief held him back and threatened his success. Each new area of your work will need many different skills. But there's something else that is even more important than skills: you need the right mindset to excel, and that mindset is supported by your belief.

To find out what your limiting beliefs are, ask yourself key questions and list the areas of your career in which you are not getting what you want. Search yourself and discover what makes you feel weak, powerless, incompetent, or held back. Conduct an internal audit and ask yourself these questions: What message am I giving to myself? Is that message worth my time? From where am I getting these messages?

My father shared a riddle with me that connected my thoughts not only to the importance of belief but also to how narrow beliefs tie us down. Let me share it with you here. A father and son are in a car crash. Both require surgery and are rushed to the hospital. The father dies. The boy is taken to an operating room and the surgeon says, "I can't operate on this boy because he's my son." Who is the surgeon and how is the boy related to the surgeon? What is your answer? Think before you read ahead.

If you struggled to think of a reasonable answer, don't beat yourself up. Confirmation bias affected your ability to uncover the correct answer. In case you're wondering, the correct answer is simple: the surgeon is the boy's mother. In hindsight, this is obvious, but it's possible that you unconsciously overlooked the possibility of a female surgeon. Instead, you searched for solutions to the problem that were wrong, but maintained your beliefs of the surgeon being male. I have shared this riddle to thousands of people in my seminars and to date no one has given me the right answer. Maybe you did. This is where our thinking narrows down and productivity becomes affected.

Productivity is vital to entrepreneurs and leaders. Unfortunately, self-limiting beliefs are deadly to anyone aspiring to enhance productivity because they lower your aspirations, create a pattern of self-sabotage, increase procrastination, and drain your energy. Most of the beliefs we hold in our professional lives are limiting beliefs. Below are a few self-limiting beliefs and solutions to counteract them. Do they resonate with you or someone whom you know?

I can't get ahead because I don't know anybody in the industry.
- A friend of mine recently invested her time and money to start up her freelance writing and editing business. She started off well but after about eight months her motivation to grow the business expired. This is because she believed she can't get ahead as she doesn't know anybody in this industry. She felt stuck. Many of us have had similar thoughts. Overcome this by getting out there, meeting people, and finding multiple channels to network.

There is no growth in my company.
- I was invited to conduct a two-day workshop at a Fortune 500 company. The session was for a team of managers and senior managers. The workshop was followed by five one-on-one coaching sessions. During the coaching, many managers spoke to me about their frustration that there is no growth in their company. They told themselves that to grow further, they had to play office politics. They could overcome this belief by dissecting the messages.

I can't count on anyone to do things as well as I can.
- Numerous business owners and corporate leaders say that they are stressed out because of their workloads. They must oversee everything because it's hard to count on their team to get things done perfectly. They doubt the capabilities of team and feel the need to be in control of everything that goes on in the company. You can overcome this by trying to raise your trust level.

It is very important for our team to have harmony.
- I once worked closely with the owner of a well-established day-care. She had a winning attitude and had a passion toward her work. She had grown her business and had 6 daycares in different cities. But, in the years since, her business growth had stagnated. She believed that for success, it is very important for all her teams to have harmony. Any incompatibility in team members was unacceptable to her. She had been tirelessly working toward maintaining continuous harmony in her team. To overcome this limiting belief she had to take a step to let go and let everyone adjust to each other's attributes.

I must know peoples hidden agenda.
- I was in a coaching session with a senior manager of a mid-size company. He was looking to get into the director role. But for a few years he was stuck in his role and couldn't see any progress. He hated to play corporate politics, but felt it may be necessary. His entire focus was to know people's hidden agenda due to which he tried his best to find out what's behind the scenes. Did it get him anywhere? Of course not! He had to overcome this by taking care of his agenda to move ahead.

All the above incidents are self-induced beliefs that stop success. This is why many feel success is limited to a lucky few. The only way to overcome self-limiting beliefs and become the lucky few who get success can be summed up in one word: action. The moment you realize you aren't getting to where you want to be because of limiting beliefs, start taking action to overcome them. Most people are completely oblivious to the power that their own beliefs have.

How you code and give meaning to your experiences shapes your beliefs. You've probably never heard of the man that I am about to share with you. However, in Hungary, he's a national hero: everybody there knows his name and his incredible story. He was the top pistol shooter in the world. He was expected to win the gold in the 1940 Olympic games scheduled for Tokyo. Those expectations vanished one terrible day just months before the Olympics. While training with his army squad, a hand grenade exploded in his right hand, and his shooting hand was blown off.

After a month in the hospital depressed, he did the unthinkable: he picked himself up, dusted himself off, and decided to learn how to shoot with his left hand! He did not let the belief that he could only shoot with his right hand stop him. For months he practiced by himself, and in the spring of 1939, he showed up at the Hungarian National Pistol Shooting Championship. Other shooters approached him to give him their condolences and to congratulate him on having the strength to come watch them shoot. They were surprised when he said, "I didn't come to watch. I came to compete." They were even more surprised when he won!

The 1940 and 1944 Olympics were cancelled because of World War II. It looked like his Olympic Dream would never have a chance to realize itself. But he kept training and in 1944 he qualified for the London Olympics. At the age of 38, he won the Gold Medal and set a new world record in pistol shooting. Four years later, he won the Gold Medal again at the 1952 Helsinki Olympics. If you haven't yet recognized him, then you may know him by his name: Karoly Takacs, a man with the self-belief to bounce back from anything. Which beliefs are you ready to drop and which will you adopt? Nothing holds you back from achieving success in your professional life except your own self. Redirect your mind and believe anew.

KARMA 17

Cherish Your Health

Health brings wealth. Without good health, you cannot succeed. Your results are because of you; you are not because of the results. You must be optimally healthy. Your health is more important than anything else. Let me tell you a story about a successful business owner named Irene that I met at a business conference in Chicago. She owned five branches of a well-known ice cream shop. Her husband owned a mobile food truck and conducted many food events. Both were dedicated to achieve their dreams.

Irene and I connected well during our initial meeting and met often over coffee and lunch. We became good friends. During our conversations, I often found Irene taking one pill after another. She said that these pills kept her anxiety level under control, and helped her reduce her back pain. She also said that the pills helped to cure the ulcers in her stomach and build up her immunity. In the process of fulfilling her dreams, she said that she lost her good health. At one time she was bubbling with health and was moving faster toward her goals. She and her husband did not even realize when health became a concern. At the age of 34 when they should have been enjoying their career life and moving with speed toward their goals, they were slowing down.

Here's another story about the need to cherish your health in business. Last year, my husband's colleague, Rajesh, a senior manager from a Fortune 500 company, suffered a heart attack at a young age. He underwent a surgery and had to be very cautious of his lifestyle thereafter. That event changed his entire life. I learnt that prior to his heart attack, he was in good health and climbing up the corporate ladder to become the director. Competition was tough as there would be only one position with numerous potential applicants from the company pool as well as from outside. To achieve his goals, he took extra responsibilities and worked night hours on global teams. He would wake up in the middle of the night, remembering an email to be sent and tasks to complete. He made it a point to respond to every office email the first thing in the morning. Food became a second priority, and junk food was his diet. Tension loomed around him at all times and slowly his health went down, leading to the heart attack. Today he is still a Senior Manager in the same company, aspiring to become the Director. His pace slowed down considerably, which has delayed his growth in the company.

At a seminar I was facilitating for women business owners and corporate leaders, a common topic of discussion was health. Most women sacrifice their health to take care of family needs at the same time that they pursue their professional careers. Most of the participants in the seminar knew the importance of maintaining their health and had memberships to gyms near their workplace. Yet, all of them felt guilty for not having the time to go to the gym to exercise.

My father always encourages me to cherish good health. My father is a man of high integrity—an intellectual who has succeeded in operating many businesses during his professional life. When I completed my business management studies and got an offer from a company in their Human Resources department, I clearly remember working around the clock to get to the level of Human Resources manager as quickly as possible. And I did. Once in that role, I worked nonstop. Unmarried and with plenty of dreams, I kept working toward my goals without taking a pause. One night my father took me to dinner at my favorite restaurant. While having dinner he casually asked me about my work and goals for future. As I excitedly told him all about it, he asked me a question: "How do you think you will achieve your goals without good health?"

My father told me that life asks you to pay a price for everything you ask of it. Was I willing to pay the price of the good health I have now? His words left a lasting impression on me. They changed my entire thought process. I realized the importance of health to achieve whatever I want to. Without it career life will be ailing. I had been neglecting the being. That day I decided to make health a priority on my daily list and it remains so today. No doubt that whatever care we take, there isn't any guarantee that health will be at its best. But at least you won't be guilty of not cherishing it. At least you know in your heart that the truth of the matter is that you have always moved ahead to make your health a priority.

There is nothing in our lives that is more valuable than good health. A healthy person sings the glory of success and is able to work hard to realize his dreams. Think about it: would you want poor health but loads of success, or would you rather have great health and keep moving ahead toward growth and success? This body and mind that we have been gifted are the most crucial instruments needed to succeed in our professional life. Yet, in an attempt to succeed and achieve, these instruments are most neglected.

Our health depends on several factors such as the food we eat, our environment, and our sleeping patterns. It involves the air we breathe, the water we drink, and the sunlight we invite into our day. Good health demands that we take note of every aspect of our lifestyle. But most of all, good health depends on our mindset. We are in an era where companies are providing the best facilities to their employees in an attempt to keep them healthy. These companies roll out multiple initiatives to boost employees' health like paid time off, healthcare packages, flex time, healthy cafeterias, and on-site doctors, and these initiatives are noble, worthy, and essential. Yet statistics show that the biggest killer worldwide (especially among executives) is the heart attack followed by diabetes.

Likewise, young entrepreneurs and aspiring leaders are also falling prey to ill health. This is because today the major emotions within a workplace are frustration, disappointment, stress, anxiety, irritation, and the crushing feeling of being overwhelmed. Even the best food diet and physical exercise can do no good if you do not take care of and exercise your mind.

We're often told that if we wish to rejuvenate our selves, then we must indulge in spas, go away for long vacations, spend time in the bathtub surrounded by aromatic candles, go shopping, and eat extravagantly. While all these make us "feel" good, the effect is frequently temporary. Soon we are back in the cycle of stress, anger, frustration, and worry at work. This is because we are focusing on the outer self (meaning, the body) and not taking care of the inner self (meaning, our thoughts, feelings, and senses).

It is very important to feed and nourish the mind. Our state of mind affects everything around us at work. For example, when your mindset is healthy, your job performance, relationships, and overall professionalism are good. But when your mindset is suffering, you cannot enjoy your career. Most of the time we feed our mind with toxic foods like negative self-criticism. We hear and read negative thoughts and then spread fear, tension, and worry. All these occupy space in your mind, clouding your ability to think appropriately. And success demands wholesome thinking and decision-making.

You may be a millionaire and the most successful person on the planet, but if you do not have peace of mind, if you can't sleep well at night, if your mind has toxic thoughts, then what good is that money and success? It'll all be spent on regaining your health. When asked what surprised him most, the Dalai Lama answered "Man. Because he sacrifices his health in order to make money. Then he sacrifices money to recuperate his health. And then he is so anxious about the future that he does not enjoy the present. The result being that he does not live in the present or the future; he lives as if he is never going to die, then dies having never really lived." When you neglect your mental well-being, it's natural to become your "own worst enemy" by harshly criticizing any mistake, and continually having a negative internal dialogue. How many of us wake up each day and say, "Today I am fortunate to be alive, and I have a precious human life, and I am not going to waste it"?

The fact that we wake up to stress, to emails, and to rushed actions throughout the day, means that we are not pausing to take care of our internal state of our mind. It is with this state of mind that you will make all decisions at your work. What do you think will be the quality of your decisions? Many religious scriptures from all over the world tell us that our mind is the most powerful instrument bestowed upon us. The physical world has limits, but our mind does not. So the only way to make full use of this instrument of success bestowed upon us by the universe itself is to give it all priority and take the utmost care of it. Stressing out about something is useless. It's like depleting the power of your mind. Mind is a seat of consciousness, thoughts, feeling, and intellectual power. Nourishing it is imperative for success. A well-nourished and peaceful mind improves work efficiency, work productivity, work relationships, and work growth. So how does one take care of the mind? Here are some quick tips that can be implemented daily.

1. **Step 1:** Become conscious of your mindset (feelings, emotions).
2. **Step 2:** Check your usual pattern of relating as you rid your mind of hurt, anger, and confused feelings.
3. **Step 3:** Observe your actions when such feelings surface.
4. **Step 4:** Switch to the feeling you would want to generate instead.
5. **Step 5:** Ask yourself how you would like to feel each day.

Most professionals that I have met said to me that there is barely any time to incorporate all of these things in their busy schedules. They are so busy that they work through lunch in spite of the knowledge that we have gained about mindful eating. It is strange that things which should be at the top of our list are not anywhere on our list. In *The Secrets of CEOs*, Steve Tappin interviewed 150 global chief executives about business and leadership. Tappin found that there are CEOs who manage to negotiate the perils of the job. He gave the example of Philip Green, the CEO of the British firm United Utilities. "He is a Christian and he has a 'five f' formula: faith, family, fitness, fun and firm," said

Tappin. "Notice he didn't say firm first. This is key to him being able to succeed."

Most of us are doing everything to achieve targets, meet deadlines, sell more products, and be a peak performer, but our internal environment continues to be full of stress, struggle, disturbances, and anxiety. In this chaotic state of mind, now do you come to work each day? How do you think of productivity when you work in a chaotic state of mind? How will the result be?

Let's turn to a story that illustrates the problem. Well-educated and successful, Karan seems to have it all. He has a Ph.D., an interesting career, and good friends. His health looks great, and he is in good shape physically. So everything's great, right? Not exactly. Karan also has high thyroid levels. He also has insomnia. And while he loves his job, he feels anxious about it. He often gets angry with himself and snaps at his team for small mistakes. It turns out that despite Karan's generally healthy habits, his anxiety and busy schedule prevented him from paying attention to the cues his body was giving him.

If you want to achieve higher results, if you want to increase productivity, if you want to create a positive work environment, you have to be healthy in your mind first. Health brings wealth. The being (self) is more important than the doing (results). Remember: Results are because of you, and you are not because of the results. Today the focus is on the results with the being facing ill health. And the cycle of ill health will continue until the realization emerges that sustainable results can flow only from a conditioned mindset. We're always running tight inside of ourselves because of sensitive workplace issues, holding on to grudges, trying to control issues, and trying to meet deadlines. We continue operating in this condition day after day with the aim of increasing productivity, of being a peak performer, of growing in the organization, of feeling fulfilled at work, of creating a positive impact. If you want to be an influential leader, it is imperative to first work on having a healthy mindset. Focus on the being first.

Health, both physical and mental, is needed for success. Each day you take to work both the body and the mind. We often focus on nourishing our physical health with fitness and food and forget that to function at our optimal level is very important to nourish the mind. The roots (mindset) must be nourished to get the fruits (results). If you nourish your mind you have the greatest resource to help keep you moving ahead even during times of distress. Professional life is full of surprises both pleasant and unpleasant. Many things that happen in your career life can disrupt your emotional health. If emotional health is weak, it weakens the immune system of the body making it more likely for you to fall sick. This has a negative impact on your productivity and growth. You want to ensure you are healthy both physically and in mind. If you work on keeping yourself physically and mentally healthy, then you will sail through your professional life smoothly. How often do you stop and think about your mind?

Years ago I met a person who was in the mid-life of his career. Because of the awareness his company had spread about health care, he took great care of his physical fitness and his food and daily routine. Yet, many times he felt that in spite of days with less work pressures, he still felt mentally drained and bored at work. Once he concentrated on taking care of his mental health, things changed for the best. Mental well-being and physical health are interconnected.

During my workshops, I talk about ways to have a healthy mindset. A healthy mindset means thinking and feeling positively. So here are the five steps to create a positive work environment as you cherish your health:

1. **Step 1:** Remove toxic people from your life. Make a list of all people around you who are negative energy drainers or who constantly disturb you emotionally. Reaching your goal requires a high level of energy and emotions, and toxic people will never allow you to keep your energy level high.

2. **Step 2:** Add wholesome people to your life. Consciously be on a look out and add people who are wholesome in their thinking and actions. These are people who are self-motivated and driven. They have a high self-esteem.

3. **Step 3:** Feed your mind daily with positive news. The news today bleeds with negativity. Take time to find positive news. Read stories of how people converted changes into success. When you read positive news at the start of the day, your mind uses this news to navigate through your daily problems.

4. **Step 4:** Spend at least 10 min in the day silently meditating for mental exercise. It is like jumpstarting your day to have a smooth day ahead.

5. **Step 5:** Mantras have great power. They are powerful thoughts that not only serve our bodies but also influence our mind, immune system, and our spirit. Some mantras that I share with my clients, which have benefitted them in their jobs, are as follows: "I am a powerful being," "I am divine," "I am the creator of my thoughts," or "I am the designer of my destiny."

When you practice these five steps, you invite positive health into your professional life. You can genuinely accomplish anything of lasting significance in your outer environment by altering your inner climate. It is said, "you are what you eat." Similarly, "You are what you think." All your actions are mind-driven. A healthy mind is a splendid treasure of ideas and possibilities. It has clarity and focus. It is emotionally stable. It can make beneficial decisions. All of these are imperative for success in any industry and role. By caring for your mind with proper thoughts and exercise you ensure lasting success and prosperity along with the ability to function at optimal level.

There is more to work life than meetings, deadlines, goals, and clients. Giving yourself at least 10 min daily of meditation sets a positive tone for your entire day, keeping your mind and body healthy. You are in control of what enters your mind. Start to reject mental junk food like negativity, boredom, loneliness, anxiety, negative television news, and worry. Instead shift to a wholesome mental diet of reading something of value daily for 15 min, of the spirit of giving, listening to inspirational podcast while traveling, meditating, spending time in silence.

The more that you make this a habit, the more ingrained it will become in the way you go throughout the day. Eventually, these small changes to your mental diet will add up in one very big way. You will become more in command of your work and thoughts. Remember: Health is wealth, and success is possible with speed and serenity.

KARMA 18

No Regrets

The starting point of all regret is within the mind. It had been 15 years since the incident took place. But even today, Heather, one of my clients, remembers it as if it happened just yesterday. Heather was young and bubbling with life when she moved up to the position of an Assistant Regional Manager at a bank. Heather and the Regional Manager were to head the North zone, which included the entire belt from Washington, DC to New York. Heather was happy for her promotion. During the course of her job, she and the female CEO of the company built healthy working relations. Both would often speak over the phone about company matters. During these conversations, Heather often shared ideas and suggestions that her CEO admired.

Conversations soon went deeper. Instead of sharing the information with the Regional Manager to whom she reported directly, Heather started to consciously bring to the CEO's attention little things done inappropriately at work. Heather knew the CEO appreciated her messages. Slowly the CEO started giving Heather more responsibility, and soon, within a year, Heather became the Regional Manager. Today Heather regrets her actions. She wants to go back in time to fix her behavior. A record plays continuously within Heather's mind, telling her that because of her actions and conversations, the CEO decided to let the existing Regional Manager go. The very thought that someone lost a job because of her makes Heather feel painful regret.

Do you ever remember that icky feeling that gnaws at you and sinks in your stomach? It's that dreaded "Good God! Oh no! What was I thinking? Why me?" Many of us regret things we've done and things we haven't. We find it easy to forgive others, but find impossible to forgive ourselves. The Roman philosopher Cato said, "I can pardon everybody's mistakes except my own." For some reason people persist in being harsh with themselves. It is said that one of the biggest ways that Satan tries to get us is to mentally disturb us with the feeling of regret.

I know a doctor who carried a lifelong sense of regret because he could not pursue his dreams of becoming a chef because his parents wished for him to pursue medicine. Regret is an emotion that all of us have felt at various times in our professional lives. But this one emotion can drain and depress, robbing us of our mental peace and energy. We regret whenever we think we should have done something, but did not do it, or whenever we should not have done something, but went ahead and did just that. All regrets emanate from the mind.

When was the last time you regretted something you did or didn't do? For me it happened about 30 min prior to typing this sentence. Instead of focusing on writing I was checking messages and emails and responding to them. But guess what, in the past two days, I was only focused on writing and did not check emails or messages and I regretted that too as I missed an important email!

In any case regret follows us. Whether you let go of an employee or keep him, whether you go that extra mile to motivate your teams or you don't, whether you watch TV or do your work, whether you invest in stocks or don't, whether you play corporate politics or you don't, whether you work hard or you don't—in all of these cases, regrets always diminish us. While on a vacation to Paris with my friend, I remember I had a list of sightseeing options I had itemized to complete within the 4 days of our trip. We were rushing from one site to another to complete it all. One evening we were sitting and enjoying the cool breeze around the beach wanting to see the sunset.

"Come on, let's go fast, the evening show is starting," I said to my friend, standing up to command her attention.

"No, let's spend more time here as we both like it. Let's see the sunset," she replied.

"Yes, but then we would miss the evening show," I anxiously answered.

"Something will always be missed. Let's enjoy where we are right now. For what we miss, we also gain something," my friend wisely said, taking my hand in hers with a smile. Her wisdom has stayed with me ever since.

Something will always be missed. For what we miss, we gain something. For every action we take in our professional life, we gain and lose something. Nature is so integrated that we don't know what we gain or lose. We don't know if a gain was truly a gain or a loss was truly a loss. While we cannot control the events that happen, we can choose how we experience these events. Think about some events in your professional life that give you a sense of regret. Now consider that it all may have happened for the good—for your good and for someone else's good.

Regret is a form of clinging. Regret can be triggered by something you did or didn't do, something another person did or didn't do, or some combination of these. You may be clinging to memories of something bad that happened to you or to regret over some action you took. This heaviness pulls you back and your speed slows down. Remember what we read earlier: success is about speed and serenity. Regret of any kind robs you of that speed and serenity.

Regret can often involve negative, self-judgmental thoughts. Words like "I should have, I wish…I could've, I would've, or I shouldn't have" become mainstays in our vocabulary, causing us to see ourselves as bad, irresponsible, undeserving, or selfish. These words are paralyzing and tormenting. They make us wish for a different past that stops us from dealing adequately with the present. We often let the choice that we didn't make weigh us down. While regret can be positive when it leads to learning, most of the time, I have noticed that regret is a devastating monster if we don't keep it in check.

The worst thing we can do when feeling regretful is to abandon our duty. I once attended a conference for policemen. At this conference, a few law enforcement officers who had completed more than 25 years of service were invited to speak about their experience. The speech that caught my attention was by an officer who shared a moment from his journey in the police force. He said the toughest part for him was when he was once confronted with a situation when he had to arrest his own relatives for felonies, knowing well that they would receive tough imprisonment. He said he felt a strong sense of guilt and was unable to decide what the right action might be. The only thought that gave him courage at that time was, "Think only of your duty and do not waver." He said he took the necessary action and arrested them. He further wisely said, "Regret would stay with me whether I had arrested them or not. But, today the magnitude of regret for arresting my relatives is much less than not arresting. I feel I have done my duty." The hall was filled with applause for him.

Psalms 6:6-7 reads, "I am weary with my moaning; every night I flood my bed with tears; I drench my couch with my weeping. My eye wastes away because of grief; it grows weak because of all my foes." Like this passage from the Bible, regret can lead to anxiety, depression, and self-denial. By choosing to experience regret, one chooses to focus on the past. The downward spiral of feeling can prevent you from progressing in your career.

Regret is an emotional warning sign. There are many situations that cause us regret during our careers. Let me share some of the most common with you:

- I regret trying to change those around me rather than changing myself to value others more.
- I regret that I often let my work take priority over my family and health.
- I regret accepting the first job offer.
- I regret allowing my boss to bully me.
- I regret being in the same job for years.
- I regret turning down a new job opportunity to stay with an employer.

- I regret I didn't pursue my passion.
- I regret I waited too long to start my business.
- I regret I did not take my career seriously.
- I regret playing it too safe.
- I regret worrying about pretty much everything at work.
- I regret not following my dream to become a doctor.
- I regret thinking too much about what other people thought of me.
- I regret not doing more of what I love.
- I regret not spending enough time on self-development.
- I regret not realizing that we are all replaceable.

Now think of one regret you have been holding on to in your work life. Then focus your mind on these 11 ways to deal with the regret:

1. Be aware of the regret and acknowledge its visit.
2. Reflect on your past but don't lament over it.
3. Remember that there is a reason for everything that has happened, is happening, and will happen. There are many things beyond your understanding.
4. Try focusing in one direction. Regret usually stems from impulsive acts and decisions.
5. Take time to choose your options every day.
6. Do not hope to make fewer mistakes. Explore and try out new things.
7. Keep moving forward.
8. Think about how far you've come.
9. Forgive yourself for a better today.
10. Focus on gratitude.
11. Learn from everything that happens to you, with you, and for you.

One of the best ways that I have found to deal with regret and convert it to opportunities is to be aware of my internal talk. Most regrets stem from your internal monologue. If left unattended the negative self-talk magnifies itself and presents to us all the things we should've and could've done to make us feel fearful and hit rock bottom in the present. Slow down those negative messages. Check if certain people, situations, or memories trigger the negative self-talk.

Regret takes away power from you. As Marsha Petrie Sue rightly said, "Stay away from what might have been and look at what can be." Constantly reminding ourselves that nothing is permanent helps us recover from regret quicker. Embrace impermanence. Everything in our career is impermanent. While you may not be happy with the actions that ended a work relationship or created a terrible situation, it's not permanent. I found it useful to keep a mantra (an affirming statement) by my side so that when I am confronted with regret at any time of the day, I can say this mantra to myself to keep me empowered to complete my day. Say, "This too shall pass," and recognition of impermanence will generate new results. There are no guarantees in life—even if you make very few mistakes.

While regret may be painful, it may also be your best friend. We can use regret to change the quality of our professional life. Regret has a message for you. Those who take regret positively have a higher degree of responsibility to do well. It drives them to be better every time, to work harder, and perform better. They even behave in certain ways that live up to the organization's expectations. Those who take regret negatively have a lower degree of responsibility to do well. They feel drained out emotionally and physically, stagnating their growth and making them feel unpleasant about themselves. Most of us allow regret to play negatively on us. It is heavy baggage that we carry to work daily.

My husband's friend works as a director at a Fortune 500 IT company. Over the years, I learned from him that he and many leaders in his organization regret having to lay off a team member. They regret giving negative feedback that lowers someone's performance rating. They regret not having spent enough time with the employee on their training. They regret not getting involved in corporate politics.

This feeling stays with them even years after it has taken place. It is then followed by regret-driven actions like avoiding to even look at workers that they feel they may have wrong. Then some do extra favors for others; become lenient on the rules of probation; or try to make it up to their employees by lowering expectations about their work. Regret may destroy management's ability to fairly hold their employees to high standards.

In the initial years of my career, when I was working as an office manager in the education industry, I remember that some parents complained about our school's customer service. After a few repeated such complaints, the head of operations for that area called a meeting with our school staff. What followed in that meeting was a flood of emotions by her. Afterward, we all felt guilt and regretted our behaviors. We needed to improve, but we did not need to emotionalize the experience to the point where we reacted negatively and blamed ourselves or others for things we did not do. We needed to positively step up to see that errors never happen again while having no regrets that held us back.

Your career life is full of decisions. From big life-altering decisions like quitting job to the smaller, everyday ones, like committing to go to that networking event instead of succumbing to the lure of your couch. The hardest part is not the decision but coping with the "what if" afterward. Any decision you take should be in the best interest of your duty. As Chapter 2, Verse 47 of the *Bhagavad Gita* reads, "You have a right to perform your duty. Never consider yourself to be the cause of the results of your action and never be attached to not doing your duty."

Having met numerous people around the globe, I observed there is one regret that almost everyone has. We regret losing time. Youth have shared with me that they regret wasting their precious teen years with frivolous pursuits like being on social media. Women tell me they regret spending hours in front of the television, which could have been used for developing themselves. I hear men and women in the professional sphere tell me they regret wasting time on negativity and gossip. To come out of the cycle of wasting time, people enroll in time management courses. But, has that done any good? I coach people to manage themselves and to become the leader of their own time. This requires mental mastery and no regrets. Keep moving ahead and you will have unstoppable success.

KARMA 19

Be Grateful

Here are some common complaints that you may have heard through-out your career:

- "I hate the traffic while commuting to work."
- "My work is so boring."
- "Work life is tedious."
- "My boss is so demanding."
- "I hate my job."
- "There are so many problems I have to deal with daily at work."
- "Life at work is routine."
- "Business life is hard."
- "The meeting consumes my energy."

You may have even said these statements yourself. Not many years ago my life revolved around these statements too. I had forgotten what it means to be thankful for having a job. Yes, at times it would dawn on me to be thankful, but those were rare instances. These complaints ignore a central truth: success demands the attitude of gratitude.

I learned the lesson of gratitude when I was invited to speak at the career fair held in my county library. At the time I was working as a Human Resources Director at a well-established company. I felt bored with the routine of work, of not growing in my career, of dealing with day-to-day work issues, and my work life seemed hard. That day when

I went to speak at the library, I was told that the participants were either young new job seekers who had never worked or laid off employees searching for jobs. I went ahead with my talk and shared tips with them about success at work. After the session, we were networking and I heard statements like

- "It must be a great feeling to be working."
- "You are lucky you survived the layoff."
- "I am willing to start off in any role; I just need a job to survive."
- "Being in the workforce must give many opportunities to explore."
- "You must be enjoying travelling and seeing the world while working."
- "You are lucky to be earning well."

As I left the library that day, something unlocked within me. I felt blessed, happy, and truly lucky to be doing what I want to do. While driving back home, there were only two words on my lips: THANK YOU.

Later, I identified this feeling of happiness as gratitude for my employment. The feeling of gratitude reduced my anger, stress, regret, frustration, and resentment. My work was still the same. I had the same problems. I still do groan when the morning alarm goes off. And yes: I did sometimes complain about work when the day dragged on or when travel stressed me out. What changed was my thinking. This change took me far in my success. The simple act of saying, "Thank you," inspired me to build healthy relations with people at work. It helped me stop groaning and complaining regularly about my workload. Changing my thinking helped me become more alert, enthusiastic, and determined compared with my peers.

I continue to be grateful for my job. Every day I start my morning with gratitude for yet another day to create a positive impact in the lives of others. Whenever I am confronted with stress and anger, I repeat this simple yet powerful two-word mantra to myself, "Thank you," and I remind myself how grateful that I am to be a part of this professional world.

Gratitude is a positive emotion that we must carry with us each day to the workplace. It's an emotion that helps us bounce back in times of adversity. Sadly, we often remember to be grateful only when we see someone else's misfortune. It is because of lack of gratitude in our daily lives that we feel job dissatisfaction, and often, burnout. The practice of gratitude is not in any way a denial of life's difficulties. Rather, gratitude is a practice that focuses the mind on being fulfilled within our careers.

One of the reasons we don't feel grateful everyday is because of the covetous nature of our culture. People crave more and more in their career life simply because of what a peer has. Coveting what others have makes you anxious and disturbs your state of mind. It makes you feel like a loser and you know the state in which a loser lives. There is nothing wrong with healthy competition or wanting more. What is not right is greed and not enjoying what we already have. My father would always say to be grateful for what you have and be extra grateful for what you do not have. He said this because there is a higher power that has our life map well planned out. If we haven't received what we want, then there may still be something good in store for us. The higher power, the universe always wishes the best for everyone.

I remember in a staff meeting, my team looked gloomy. Before starting off with our agenda, I gave them a piece of paper and asked them to write down anonymously what problems they have in life, both personal and professional. I then had them fold it and put it in a basket. I jumbled them up and then asked them to take one paper out of the basket and read it to themselves. When everyone finished reading the new set of problems from the paper they picked, I asked, "How many of you would like to have your own problems back versus how many would like to keep the new set of problems." All of them agreed that they would prefer to have their problems back. This exercise changed everyone's mood and perception. While they were reading others' problems, they felt blessed that their problems weren't as bad as they imagined.

So how can you practice gratitude in your regular life to help you get closer to your desired outcome? Here are two simple steps I often share with my clients:

- **Step 1:** Count your blessings. I know you've heard this statement countless times. But have you practiced it countless times? Be honest here. Have you been grateful for the difficult times in your career life because they are shaping up and making you stronger than you ever wanted to be?
- **Step 2:** Make each day count. Have you waiting for Thanksgiving or that perfect situation to give thanks? Every day counts when being grateful. Well, the fact that you are alive and healthy is the biggest reason to be grateful. Because you are on your feet you can make a great impact today. You have an opportunity that some were denied.

In the first book of Thessalonians 5:18 of the Bible says, "In everything give thanks." What seems initially unfortunate may turn out to be blessing. So give thanks for whatever is happening in your life right now at this moment. We enter the professional world with lots of hope and confidence to grow. Then the routine nature of our jobs converts hope and confidence into fear and doubts. It's pretty easy to take our jobs for granted. We forget that there are many people out there who would do just about anything to be in our shoes.

Gratitude is a mindset, a positive emotion, and a practice that when unleashed completely opens the door to more opportunities and better relationships. It calms the mind, increases energy, reduces stress, and raises productivity. Be grateful to your job and magnify that gratitude to others so they too learn the great importance of gratitude in our working lives.

KARMA 20

Check Your Baggage

My work takes me around the globe. Every time I travel, I have to be extra mindful about the weight of my luggage. Most airlines require carry-on and stowed items to be below a certain weight. International travel has the most severe requirements for luggage weight. Overall, whether you are travelling in the country or internationally, the rule of the thumb is to travel light. This means you have to be very selective about what goes into the baggage. This mindfulness carries over into your daily working life: as you progress through your career, travel easy. Check your baggage daily. Know what's going into it and know what's coming out of it. Travel light. Let the things that weigh you down go.

As we spend more time in our careers, we start filling our minds with experiences, lessons, and conditioned responses. Our "travel bag" becomes filled with negativity, doubt, stress, politics, professional grudges, anxiety, pressure, bad experiences, regret, guilt, and desire. There are items like happiness and passion in the bag, but they are few. With time, knowingly or unknowingly, the bag becomes bigger and heavier. We don't put this bag down. And most of us will carry it until we exit our career life, and maybe even later. It becomes a part of us.

This is why today there are so many courses and lectures on stress management. We feel stress is coming from outside, and hence, most of the courses teach us how to deal with stress outwardly. Stress will persist until we realize that it is created by us. Our mental baggage is becoming heavier, and we have to first approach it internally. The rule of thumb for career success is to travel light. It is not just the weight of the baggage but also what's inside the baggage. The quality and quantity both are important.

Luke 6:45 of the Bible says, "A good person produces good things from the treasury of a good heart, and an evil person produces evil things from the treasury of an evil heart. What you say flows from what is in your heart." Often your success depends on what's in your baggage. If there is anger in the baggage, you will be disturbed at even the slightest issue at your workplace, and you will make irrational decisions leading to failure. If you have happiness in your baggage, you will move ahead and find solutions to all obstacles, leading to your success. Failure and success are a matter of your internal state rather than external environment.

Another thing I have often witnessed is that people carry excess baggage. Excess work, excess negativity, excess stress, and excess grudges. Excess baggage complicates your work and your mind. Don't accumulate it if you don't need it. It will only make you feel heavier and slow you down. Overweight baggage has a price you pay. If your mental bag is overfilled with negativity, then that is what you will deliver negative results.

A successful human resource manager was great at his operational tasks at work. However, his relationship with his team, peers, and upper management was problematic. He distrusted people around him and always felt that people were out to stab him in the back. Every time he had an idea or plan, he resisted the thought of sharing it with his team. He would feel that they would use his ideas and present them as their own. Because of this behavior, his growth had slowed down, and he was always stressed at work. As an executive coach, one of my most important roles is to help my clients understand what they are bringing to work each day. So when I coached this human resource manager, it was clear that he was bringing elements from his personal life to his work life and things were getting entangled at work.

Most of us drag our unresolved family hurt with us to relationships with peers and significant others. The baggage we carry isn't always our own. Oftentimes, we carry other people's baggage. Let me give you another example. Joshua was a health-care coach who met many clients in a week and coached them toward their well-being. When I worked with him, I have found that Joshua felt low and tired. One of the main reasons he said he was tired is that he often carries his client's baggage with him. Their issues, emotions, feelings, and words stay with him, and he keeps thinking about it. This drains him, and he isn't able to give his best at his work.

Here's another example—an old story that illustrates these lessons about carrying problematic baggage. A senior monk and a junior monk were traveling together. At one point, they came to a river with a strong current. As the monks were preparing to cross the river, they saw a very young and beautiful woman also attempting to cross. The young woman asked if they could help her cross to the other side. The two monks had taken vows not to touch a woman. Without a word, the older monk picked up the woman, carried her across the river, placed her gently on the other side, and carried on with his journey. The younger monk couldn't believe what had just happened. After rejoining his companion, he was speechless, and three hours passed without a word between them. Finally, the younger monk addressed his older monastic companion.

"As monks, we are not permitted to touch a woman. How could you then carry that woman on your shoulders?"

"Brother, I set her down on the other side of the river three hours ago," replied the older monk looking sharply at his younger friend and he continued: "Why are you still carrying her?"

Similar to the monk in this story, we carry around past confusions and hurts until we only hurt ourselves. When someone carries baggage of a past event, they trend to project all of their experiences and fears on to the present events of their lives.

Let go of the stuff that is weighing you down. Become consciously aware of the things inside your mental baggage. Ask yourself if your mind progressing or regressing? Enhance the quality of your life by reducing the quantity of your mental baggage. Do this with a simple "ABC" plan-of-action:

- **Audit:** Think for a few minutes about what is inside your mental baggage. How much is negative and how much is positive? Conduct a self-audit.
- **Blot out:** Now sort out what you don't need from this. Do you absolutely need doubts, grudges, anger, and stress in your career journey, or is it possible for you to move ahead without them? Can you add more of happiness, passion, and calm?
- **Cue your consciousness:** Now that you know what is inside your mind baggage and you have blotted out what's unnecessary, become conscious every single day of what you put inside your mental baggage.

Now that your inner baggage has been packed so thoughtfully, you will be able to tirelessly go a long way on your journey to success. Because you are travelling light and the mind is not heavy, you can cross obstacles and reach your goals with speed and serenity. A light kite flies high.

KARMA 21

Attract What You Want

I meet numerous professionals in corporations, medium-sized organizations, and small businesses around the globe. Some long for success, yet, after working hard, they fail to achieve what they want. On the other hand, other leaders and entrepreneurs quickly build thriving businesses and move from one success to the next. How is that possible? Everyone wants to achieve their goals and make it big, but only few achieve greatness. What is missing?

I've found that one of the differences lies in how some professionals break free from the things that hold them back while others don't. I've learned plenty of valuable lessons before I encountered successes that led up to founding my company. It's not just about our expertise. I truly believe that practicing incremental changes to your mind—our inner actions—is what helps us achieve our goals in this limited time that we all have in our careers.

Much has been spoken and written about the law of attraction. If it is true that you get what you attract, if people in the sports arena are vouching for this principle, if quantum physics is proving it, if healing practitioners are using it, then what stops us from using it in our careers as business professionals and leaders? American leaders like Will Smith, Oprah, Steve Harvey, and Jim Carrey have given many interviews about how they used law of attraction for their success. Yet, many in the business world still tell me that they rarely operationalize this principle, and they rarely get what they want.

We often get what we don't want in our careers: lack of growth, unhappiness, conflict, discord, lack of client's anger, irritation, a bad boss, poor work relationships, and slow business. Where has the law of attraction gone wrong for us in the business world? Why aren't we able to attract what we want in our careers? Is there something we missed while reading interviews and books about the law of attraction? Or, is it simply that we feel we are too smart and busy to even look into this aspect for success?

I remember a story I heard when I was a kid. One day, a traveler was passing through a desert. After walking for a few miles, he felt tired, hungry, and thirsty. "How I wish I could rest for a while under a tree!" he thought. Suddenly, he saw a tree in front of him! He was surprised as he was in a desert, and just a few seconds ago, there was no trace of even a bush. But at the same time he felt glad that he had a place to rest for a while. As the traveler sat under the tree, he thought, "How I wish I had water to drink!"

Just then he found a tumbler full of cold water kept on a stone in front of him. After a few minutes, the traveler thought, "How I wish I had something to eat!" In an instant, a variety of delicious food appeared before him. All that food made him wish for a bed, and he got one too! Stretching himself comfortably of the soft mattress, the traveler thought, "I wish I had someone to massage my feet." Instantly, a young man appeared and started massaging his feet and legs.

Tired as he was, the traveler soon fell fast asleep. Actually, he was under the shade of the "Wishing Tree": whoever was under it could have whatever he wished for! After a long nap when the traveler woke up, he saw the man still sitting beside his feet. Now the traveler began to think, "I am sure this is a magical part of the desert." He wondered, "Could there be a demon around too?"

Suddenly, a demon appeared.

"Are you going to eat me up?" he asked the demon.

"Yes! Get ready!" replied the demon, pouncing on the traveler.

The frightened traveler took to his heels and ran away.

Now in reality we don't see this wishing tree around us at our workplace. In principle, we can carry a wishing tree within us all the time. But to do this we must correct a mistake in our thinking. Most people's mistake in trying to apply the law of attraction is this: they long for things or they demand things. You don't attract what you long for by demanding it. Rather, you attract what you *are*. And what are you? You are the mind, body, soul, and emotion. You bring all these four elements with you to your workplace, and you can attune these four elements within yourself daily to attract the best. The foundation on which the law of attraction works is alignment of all our four elements.

Yet, it's only when our mind, body, emotions, and soul align with one another that we are able to attract what we want. Once you know how to align these, you will attract what you want. But the first step is to get to the root and understand what you are. In today's work era, tension is considered natural. I hear professionals tell me that tension is always there at work. It's a part of a career. I have met many people who tell me that stress is the driving force to achieve goals. They say it's good to have stress because it acts like adrenaline that gives you a rush to achieve.

But, when the mind is tense, you are tense. From what we read in earlier chapters, we have understood that our thoughts create energy and according to our energy level we focus on the task, finally leading to results. A mind that is filled with thoughts of tension will create what type of results? Answer: stressful results. We want happiness and great results, but we are full of tension and stress. Below are a sample goal and the problematic thoughts associated with them.

- **Goal:** I want to earn at least 1 million dollars. I want to become the CEO of the company. I want to start my own business. I want that next promotion. I want to attain a leadership role. I want to feel happier at work. I want to increase business profit. I want to grow my business operations.
- **Thoughts:** Is it possible? Can I do it? Will it be worth the time and efforts? What if I don't succeed? What if I am wrong? Maybe I am not good enough. Suppose my ideas are of poor quality.

In this instance, do you see how our goals are powerful, but our thoughts are weak? Should powerful and weak thoughts exist together? Answer: no. Do you remember as kids how we would blow bubbles with that soapy solution and then we would try to pop them with our finger? How we enjoyed doing that! As adults, even now we enjoy blowing bubbles. The difference is we now blow out bubbles of thought. Most of them are made of negative solutions. And sometimes we aren't popping them away. These same thoughts flow into the universe and eventually bubble back up within us if we don't keep popping them.

How often have you told yourself that I want a friendly and motivated team at work whether for your business or your corporate job? Now look at the kind of team member or team leader that you are. Are you a micromanager, judgmental, critical, controlling, and doubtful of people and their behaviors? Are you controlling or appreciative? Do you trust people, praising them and motivating them? If you don't have these latter qualities, then despite all of your policies and procedures, you may not attract the friendly and motivated team that you want.

Here's another way to operationalize the law of attraction by focusing on how you *are* instead of what you want or demand. Have you noticed that, when you are stressed out, the heart speeds up without any demonstrable physical activity? Next time you find yourself with negative thoughts, doubts, and feelings, take note of your physical posture. It is likely that your shoulders are slumped, spine bent, walk tense, breathing labored, and eyes cast downward. You've likely never seen someone looking down at the ground with such a posture stating enthusiastically, "I feel so energetic!" And you may have never seen someone with a straight spine, shoulders back, eyes looking upward, saying, "I feel so sad!" First think positively. Then modify your physical countenance in a way that reflects the positivity of your inner thoughts. The way you feel and what you experience in your body comes from your thoughts.

You have to be clear about the outcome and the purpose for your actions. Most of the times we are complaining: we tell ourselves of what we don't what. I don't want a rude boss. I don't want business to go down. I don't want to get into debt. I don't want to struggle in a career. When you say what you don't want, you bring your mind and body down into a negative state: frowning, slouching, and pouting. And once again you are back into the cycle where you don't get your desired results.

To attract what you want, know that the law of attraction is a combination of various universal laws and do not often operate independently:

- **Law of acceptance:** Acceptance is about trusting yourself to rise to whatever occasion presents it to you. If it happens, it happens. Go on about your business. Keep flowing. You cannot control circumstances from the outside.

- **Law of responsibility:** You are responsible for your actions. As leaders, we often forget this law toward success. We blame situations and people and thereby come in our own way of success. To be angry is to visit the faults of others on ourselves. Success or achievement is not the final goal. A successful person is one who can lay a firm foundation with the bricks that others throw at him.

- **Law of detachment:** As leaders, learn to let go and watch. What this means in business is that you must remove yourself from all personal attachment to the outcome. Sounds counter-intuitive, I know. After all, in business we are judged every day, every month, and every year by our numbers and yes, we want results. The law of detachment goes hand in hand with the law of attraction. Do everything in your power to activate the law of attraction for what you want, but don't forget to detach as if you had already received what you want. Do the best and leave the rest.

- **Law of focus:** As leaders and entrepreneurs, you have a lot on your plate. Staying focused can be tough with a constant stream of employees, clients, emails, and phone calls demanding your attention. So focus on what you want: a successful team, more clients, and happy customers. Take off your mind from all negativity as you climb up the ladder of success.

- **Law of silence:** We are conditioned to believe that when the person you are speaking to suddenly falls silent it may reflect disinterest, a breakdown of communication, or even rejection by the other person. To break our discomfort, and the silence, we quickly continue the conversation. But the "sounds of silence" are very powerful. Be intuitively aware of the power of silence and become very comfortable when this happens during the conversation. In the breaking of this silence, we may be breaking good things like concentration, reflection, and contemplation!

- **Law of self-governance:** What is ahead of you is more important than what is behind you. A mind that has forgotten the past and the future, that is awake to the now, to the present, expresses the highest concentration of intelligence. It is alert, it is watchful, and it is inspired. The actions of a person who has such a mind are exceptionally creative and powerful.

- **Law of clarity:** Be exceptionally clear about what you want and what you are. Do not just say I want to grow my network or earn more money. Have clarity. Say, for example, or write, "I want to grow my network by adding 50 more Human Resource professionals from Fortune 500 companies by December 2020."

Thoughts equal destiny. Saint Augustine said, "Faith is to believe what you do not see; the reward of this faith is to see what you believe." And Mark 11:23 of the Bible says, "Truly I tell you, if anyone says to this mountain, 'Go, throw yourself into the sea,' and does not doubt in their heart but believes that what they say will happen, it will be done for them."

That's how the Law of Attraction works. Be exceptionally clear and focus your thoughts, feelings, and actions on exactly what you want. Be focused about who you are. Be specific about what success looks like so that when it's achieved, it becomes unstoppable.

Conclusion: Celebrate

You've come so far. You've worked so hard. You've applied so many methods. You've operationalized so many principles. You've paid attention to so many karmas—the actions that animate your success. In the midst of all of these things, be sure to do one more vital act: celebrate! Celebrate at the beginning, the middle, and the end of every day. Make celebration an ongoing, unstoppable endeavor so that your beginning is your end and your ending your beginning. Visualize everlasting success and celebrate that image all the time.

Many people whom I have met tell me that their mornings invariably start with anxious, worrying exclamations like this:

- "Oh God! I have to go to work!"
- "I have a task to complete!"
- "I hate doing meetings!"
- "If I have to do one more project!"
- "Oh no! Not another email—it's so early in the morning!"

Remember: Everything that you have with you today is temporary and can be destroyed within a fraction of a second. Rather than starting your day with complaints, be grateful for what you have and celebrate each day.

Our careers are full of ups and downs. Every human being has to go through success and failure. You will face both the good and bad times. Never give up. Just because someone is ahead of you does not mean that they will win. Things can take a turn any moment. Career is a game of luck or chance, representing some higher power's rules.

The most significant lesson I learned that indeed helped me achieve my goals and dreams was that, at the end of the day, it's not the number of success or failures that you face in your career that determines your fate. Rather, your future in this game called career is defined by one thing, and one thing only: movement. Just keep moving. Don't stop. Just keep moving.

You have the power to change your future by what you do in the present moment. This is purely because you have the power to choose. You have the power to choose your thoughts. You have the power to choose your state of mind. Whatever you decide to choose leads you to take action. The universe responds to you, sooner or later, according to the quality of your actions.

The best you can do is to condition your mindset to deliver the best karmas possible. Whatever the result, let the being triumph. When you calibrate the mindset and karmas, profits, growth, and success follow automatically. All we can do is work on ourselves.

Take a moment now and ask yourself, when was the last time you celebrated? Then look ahead to the end of today and tomorrow and make all your moments full of rejoicing. The 21 karmas in this book condition your mindset for unstoppable success. Rejoice as you practice them! Whatever the result, let your being claim victory.

When you calibrate the mindset and karmas, success follows automatically because you have shaped yourself to be successful even in the toughest of times. All we can do is work on ourselves. Your body generates action, your mind generates thought, your soul generates intent, and your emotions generate feelings. You bring all of these elements to your work daily.

Never be in too much of a hurry to reach the end of the game. Enjoy the game to the fullest. No matter how beautiful the career world is everything has a shelf life. There will be a day and time when it will all end.

And as you celebrate yourself, I celebrate you. This book is dedicated to the success within you because my entire life is about offering vital tools and counsel to uplift leadership through mind. With every word, I affirm you; with every thought, I celebrate you; and with every hope, I rejoice in your triumph! Look within. It's all your karma.

Index

Printed in the United States
By Bookmasters